THE MIDDLE EAST OIL DECADE
AND BEYOND

THE MIDDLE EAST OIL DECADE AND BEYOND

ESSAYS IN POLITICAL ECONOMY

GAD G. GILBAR
University of Haifa and
Moshe Dayan Center, Tel Aviv University

FRANK CASS
LONDON • PORTLAND, OR

First Published in 1997 in Great Britain by
FRANK CASS & CO. LTD.
Newbury House, 900 Eastern Avenue
London, IG2 7HH

and in the United States of America by
FRANK CASS
c/o ISBS, 5804 N.E. Hassalo Street
Portland, Oregon, 97213-3644

British Library Cataloguing in Publication Data:

A catalogue record for this book is available
from the British Library

ISBN 0-7146-4734-9

Library of Congress Cataloging-in-Publication Data:

A catalog record for this book is available
from the Library of Congress

Printed in Great Britain by
Bookcraft (Bath) Ltd, Midsomer Norton, Avon

In memory of
Wolfgang Markus

Contents

Contents

Contents

Tables

Figures and Illustrations

Figures

Illustrations

Abbreviations

AAS	*Asian and African Studies*
ARE	Arab Republic of Egypt
CAPMAS	Central Agency for Public Mobilisation and Statistics (Cairo)
CBS	Central Bureau of Statistics (Jerusalem)
DESIPA	Department for Economic and Social Information and Policy Analysis
DK	Dawlat al-kuwayt
DS	Department of Statistics (Amman)
EIU	Economist Intelligence Unit
ESCWA	Economic and Social Commission for Western Asia
GDP	Gross Domestic Product
GNP	Gross National Product
HKJ	The Hashemite Kingdom of Jordan
IBRD	International Bank for Reconstruction and Development
IJMES	*International Journal of Middle East Studies*
IMF	International Monetary Fund
J'AS	al-Jumhuriyya al-'arabiyya al-suriyya
JPS	*Journal of Palestine Studies*
JSGAS	*Judaea, Samaria and Gaza Area Statistics*
MECS	*Middle East Contemporary Survey*
MEED	*Middle East Economic Digest*
MEJ	*Middle East Journal*
MENA	Middle East News Agency
MES	*Middle Eastern Studies*
MTM	*Marchés Tropicaux et Méditerranéens*

OAPEC	Organization of Arab Petroleum Exporting Countries
PE	*Petroleum Economist*
PLO	Palestine Liberation Organization
SAI	*Statistical Abstract of Israel*
SY	*Statistical Yearbook*
UNCTAD	United Nations Conference on Trade and Development
UNDP	United Nations Development Programme
UNFPA	United Nations Fund for Population Activities
UNIDO	United Nations Industrial Development Organization
UNRWA	United Nations Relief and Works Agency for Palestine Refugees in the Near East
USAID	United States Agency for International Development
WB	World Bank

Preface

The sudden huge price hikes in Middle Eastern oil following the October War of 1973 yielded, almost overnight, an enormous flow of resources to states and societies that could not have anticipated such instant affluence. To this came unprecedented political power because of the total control the oil states were able to maintain over oil production and prices until the second half of 1982. Thus, though covering barely nine years, the period may appropriately be dubbed "the oil decade."

Of the major changes the oil decade brought about some were quite unforeseen — e.g., the revolution that took place in the educational system of the Arab states or the change in their attitude toward establishing economic ties with Israel — while others were more predictable, such as the entrenchment of separate territorial Arab states in a move away from pan-Arabism and the growing economic and political involvement of the United States in the region.

This book highlights three fundamental aspects of the oil decade. First is the influence the production, export and revenues of oil had on domestic, regional and international relations, in particular between foreign producer companies and local governments (chapter 1); between producer governments and consumer governments (chapters 2 and 3); and between Arab producer states and Arab non-oil states (chapter 4).

Second is the expansion of higher education, no doubt the most single significant social change the oil decade engendered. Many new universities throughout the Arab world began opening their doors to an ever-increasing number of students, especially in the sciences and civil engineering. Significant was also the proportion of women students enrolling. The huge investments required for establishing advanced systems of higher learning were of course provided by the financial resources the oil states now had at their disposal, but the impetus came from the realization that only through successfully developing their human resources could they hope to transform their economic structures.

The third aspect is the way economic relations developed between the Arab states and Israel. As of the early 1970s the official Arab boycott on goods manufactured in Israel was increasingly being circumvented and a wide range of agricultural and industrial products were beginning to find their way to customers in Arab states. This was to prove of much significance when, following the first Oslo agreement of 1993, trade relations became overt and official. While there were many reasons why during this period the Arab states began quietly ignoring an economic boycott they demanded strict adherence to officially, the abrupt huge rise in the demand for industrial and consumer goods in the Arab oil states after 1973 is certainly among the dominant ones.

Chapter 2 was first published, in slightly different form, in Haim Shaked and Itamar Rabinovich (eds.), *The Middle East and the United States*, New Brunswick and London: Transaction Books, 1980, pp. 209–40, and chapter 4 in Elie Kedourie and Sylvia G. Haim (eds.), *Essays on the Economic History of the Middle East*, London: Frank Cass, 1988 pp. 196–211. The Introduction appeared first in *The Middle East Contemporary Survey* 10 (1986): 246–57. They are here reprinted with permission.

My deep gratitude is extended to Amatzia Baram, Sylvia Haim, Itamar Rabinovich and P.J. Vatikiotis for their valuable comments. I am also indebted to Judy Krausz, Dick Bruggeman, Iris Fruchter and Onn Winckler for their help in preparing this book for publication. Finally, I wish to express my thanks to two institutions for their generous support: the study of the development of higher education in seven Arab states was funded by the S. Neaman Institute for Advanced Studies in Science and Technology, Israel Institute of Technology; and research on the informal trade relations between Israel and the Arab states was made possible through a grant from the Tami Steinmetz Center for Peace Research, Tel Aviv University.

Introduction

The Oil Decade in Perspective

Following the 16 October 1973 announcement by the ministers
of the Organization of Petroleum Exporting Countries (Opec) of
their decision to double the prices of all types of crude oil, it
was widely held that a profound social and economic change was
about to occur in many societies, both developing and developed.
The Middle East oil-producing countries in particular hoped that
a new era had begun, and that as it progressed, fundamental
changes would occur in their economic and political circumstances.
There were even those who envisaged an "oil century," with
the economic and political world order being determined by the
leading members of Opec. However, the period in which the
oil states enjoyed great economic and political power terminated
in the 1980s. Retrospectively, the years 1973-82 are considered
the "oil decade," during which the economic power and political
influence of the oil states rose to incomparable heights.

The surge in economic power was predicated, of course, on
the steep rise in revenues from the export of crude oil, natural
gas and refined products. Income from oil exports by the seven
Middle Eastern members of Opec rose from $10 billion in 1972 to
a peak of $217 billion in 1980 (current prices). The total revenue
of these governments in the decade under discussion amounted
to $1,120 billion (current prices).[1] The immensity of this sum
may be gauged by the example of Saudi Arabia in 1981, when
oil revenues reached a peak of $113.2 billion, a figure which was
4.7 times greater than the Egyptian GDP that year and 5.5 times
the Israeli GDP.[2]

1

The increased political power of the Middle East oil states derived largely from the tremendous increase in their economic resources. Petrodollars bought friends and in many cases mitigated hostility in the region and elsewhere. In addition, these countries became an important market for the industrialized economies and very welcome customers at Western money markets. Above all, the dependence of Western Europe, Japan and the United States on the import of Middle East oil gave the exporters remarkable political leverage. In 1976, oil from Middle East Arab states constituted about 70 percent of France's total oil imports, 56 percent of Japan's, and 8 percent of the American total.[3]

The changes that Middle East countries underwent during the oil decade as a result of the unexpected influx of capital and international political power may be divided into three areas: (1) demographic; (2) economic and social; and (3) political.

DEMOGRAPHIC DEVELOPMENTS

Directly or indirectly, the economic forces generated by the "oil effect" gave rise to a number of demographic processes in the oil states themselves and in several neighboring countries. Three developments in this context are especially noteworthy.

The first is accelerated settlement of nomads in the Arab oil-producing countries, especially in Saudi Arabia. While at the end of the 1960s nomads were estimated as accounting for about 50 percent of the Saudi population, some 12 years later this figure had fallen to 10 percent.[4] A relatively small proportion of the beduin settled in villages, which accorded with the official policy of nomad settlement, but most headed for the main cities of the Saudi kingdom, the result of powerful pull forces generated by the rapid economic development of the major urban centers. The dramatic fall in the proportion of nomads in the total Saudi population had many consequences, the most important of which was the continued decline of tribal power in the political system.

The second development, related to the first, is the accelerated process of urbanization begun prior to the oil decade. Migration to the cities, however, was only partially connected with the settlement of nomads. It became a widespread phenomenon not only in the desert oil states, such as Saudi Arabia and Libya, but in other oil countries as well, such as Iran and Iraq. The proportion of city dwellers in the total population increased in Saudi Arabia from 30 percent in 1960 to 69 percent in 1982; in Libya from 23 to 58 percent; in Iran from 32 to 52 percent; and in Iraq from 4 to 70 percent, respectively.[5] In these, as in other Middle East oil countries, urban dwellers became the majority component of the population during the oil decade.

The third development during this period was the accelerated movement of workers among the Arab states, namely from the poor states — Egypt, Yemen (North and South), Sudan, Syria and Jordan — to the oil-rich states — Iraq, Saudi Arabia, Kuwait, Libya and the United Arab Emirates. At the peak of this process, in 1982, the number of migrant workers was estimated at about five million,[6] most of them remaining in the oil countries for only a limited number of years. This large-scale movement was prompted by the need for more workers by the oil states, whether in the context of their extensive development programs (Saudi Arabia, Libya, Kuwait) or to replace local manpower recruited into the army (Iraq). The migrant workers transferred large sums of money back to their families in their home countries, with billions of dollars reaching the poorer Arab states annually in this way. For several of these countries such transfers became a major source of foreign currency revenues. In Egypt, official transfers amounted to about $3 billion annually in the early 1980s; in Jordan, a sum of $900 million flowed in; and in Syria, the figure was $700-800 million in both 1981 and 1982.[7] The movement of workers on so large a scale from one Arab country to another, and the transfer of such large sums of money, created genuine interdependence, particularly between the rich and the poor economies, for the first time since these states were established. Any sudden drop in the scale of the transfers would severely damage the ability of such states as Egypt, Jordan and Syria to balance their foreign currency expenditures, as was proven later on. Beyond economic relations, the inter-Arab migratory movement created reciprocal ties and influences in the social and cultural spheres as well.

ECONOMIC AND SOCIAL CHANGES

The enormous amount of resources at the disposal of the oil economies following October 1973 permitted them to simultaneously increase both private and public consumption and investment by tens and sometimes hundreds of percent annually. The rise in expenditure on consumption from the mid-1970s, particularly among the upper strata, is a matter of record. Consumption by the rulers of the oil states, their families and relatives symbolized their wealth in their view. This spending was restricted only by the limits of Middle Eastern imagination and Western technology. Consumption by the other strata increased greatly as well. The volume of imported food, clothing and durable goods rose by hundreds of percent in the period under study, with a considerable proportion of these items acquired by the middle and even lower classes.

In the area of public consumption, the leap in military spending, especially in weapons acquisition, was especially marked. Iran under the Shah, Saudi Arabia, Iraq (even before the outbreak of war in 1980) and Libya each spent billions of dollars annually on sophisticated weaponry produced in the United States, other Western countries and the Soviet Union.[8] Spending on public administration also rose substantially as a result of the expansion of the bureaucratic systems in the oil countries. Investments of tens of billions of dollars were also made by each of the oil states in hundreds of development projects, although no structural change occurred in any of these countries' economies. Such a change would have been manifested, inter alia, by a noticeable drop in the relative share of the oil sector in the GDP and a parallel rise in the relative share of the non-oil sectors, primarily industry. A decrease in dependency on oil revenues did in fact become one of the major economic goals of the oil states.

However, except for the petrochemical industry, which expanded rapidly and was also primarily export-oriented, development in both light and heavy industry was limited. At the end of the oil decade, no industrial sector contributed as much as 20 percent of the GDP or employed a similar percentage of local workers. Iran alone approached this figure, its industrial production (excluding oil) constituting about 15 percent of the GDP at the end of the Pahlavi period.[9] However, a change in the structure of the Iranian economy had begun as far back as the 1930s, receiving a significant impetus during the oil decade. Of the many reasons for the failure of the Arab oil economies to bring about internal structural change, the most significant was the absence of incentives for the establishment of wide-ranging industries. In countries where foreign currency revenues were so great, and which were subject for most of the period to pressure by the industrialized economies

4

to recycle their revenues, inter alia through the massive acquisition of manufactured goods, incentives for local manufacturing were lacking. Inasmuch as none of the Arab oil countries had a policy of restrictive imports, there were virtually no administrative restrictions or import quotas that could serve as a barrier to protect local production. Any decrease in dependence on oil revenues through the growth of the non-oil sectors was therefore only marginal.

At the same time, marked and important changes did occur in two areas: the development of physical infrastructures, especially in the desert oil states, and the development of human resources, that is, investment in educational systems.

Within the space of a few years, states such as Saudi Arabia, Libya and the United Arab Emirates developed comprehensive, high-quality road networks, transportation systems, communication networks, power stations and electricity grids. These and other oil states also invested heavily in public construction and in housing, and new cities were built.[10] Priority was given by the rulers of these states to investment in infrastructure since such investment was essential for the devleopment of other economic sectors. Furthermore, whatever obstacles existed in the way of infrastructure construction, i.e., highways, airports, hospitals or schools, were speedily surmounted by government intervention. The problem of scarcity of labor was solved by opening the gates of these countries to workers, both skilled and unskilled, from abroad, while shortages of raw materials or any necessary supplies were rectified through imports. The planning and implementation of complex projects did not present a problem either, as multinational corporations from the United States, Japan and Western Europe eagerly competed over contracts for this work.

Perhaps the most impressive change occurred in the area of educational systems (see table I.1). Highly impressive sums, both in absolute and relative terms, were allocated to this development area. Saudi Arabia spent over $9 billion, and Kuwait and Libya over $1 billion each on the development and running expenses of educational systems in 1982 alone.[11] Funds were allotted not only for the construction of school buildings and the acquisition of equipment, but also for the import of teachers from Western and neighboring Arab countries. Similarly, governments subsidized the tuition fees of its nationals studying at colleges and universities in Europe and the United States. The high priority for education

5

Table I.1

Twelve Arab countries: enrollment rates for the first, second and third levels of education, 1970–82 (various years; in percentage)

Country	Year	First level	Second level	Third level
Egypt		(6-11)	(12-17)	(20-24)
	1970	72	34	8.0
	1975	73	43	13.7
	1981	78	54	14.7
Sudan		(7-12)	(13-18)	(20-24)
	1970	38	7	1.2
	1975	47	14	1.5
	1981	52	18	2.0
Bahrain		(6-11)	(12-16/17)	(20-24)
	1970	102	54	1.8
	1975	96	52	2.4
	1980	101	58	5.8
Iraq		(6-11)	(12-17)	(20-24)
	1970	69	24	5.2
	1975	94	35	9.0
	1982	109	55	10.1
Jordan		(6-11)	(12-17)	(20-24)
	1981	103	77	31.6
Kuwait		(6-9)	(10-17)	(20-24)
	1970	89	65	3.7
	1975	93	67	9.1
	1982	91	77	15.4

		(5-9)	(10-16)	(20-24)
Lebanon	1970	119	40	23.7
	1981	118	58	28.3

		(6-11)	(12-17)	(20-24)
Oman	1975	44	1	—
	1982	74	21	—

		(6-11)	(12-17)	(20-24)
Qatar	1970	102	39	
	1975	111	54	4.2
	1982	116	74	16.5

		(6-11)	(12-17)	(20-24)
Saudi Arabia	1970	45	12	1.7
	1975	58	22	4.1
	1981	67	32	8.7

		(6-11)	(12-17)	(20-24)
Syria	1970	78	38	9.2
	1975	96	43	12.1
	1981	101	48	16.0

		(6-11)	(12-17)	(20-24)
UAE	1970	98	22	—
	1975	102	33	—
	1982	102	67	6.8

Source:
UNESCO, *SY* 1984, pp. III-20-71, table 3.2.

7

was the outcome of a "rapid growth" strategy adopted by rulers and governments once they committed themselves to modernizing their economy and society.

The results of investment in educational systems were impressive, particularly the expansion of the systems of higher education and the large increase in the enrollment rates of pupils in secondary schools (i.e., the percentage of pupils attending secondary schools within the total relevant age group). In Saudi Arabia during 1970-82 this rate rose from 12 percent to 32 percent, in Iraq from 24 to 55 percent, and in the United Arab Emirates from 22 to 67 percent. Illiteracy rates also decreased consistently as a direct result of increased enrollment in primary schools. In 1982, enrollment rates in primary schools reached 67 percent in Saudi Arabia, 91 percent in Kuwait, and 97 percent in Iran.[12]

The massive influx of economic resources into the oil economies naturally affected the mode of distribution of capital and income. Existing data indicate that certain social groups and strata improved not only their real but also their relative economic condition. First, the ruling elites in the Arab oil states and in Iran until the Islamic revolution registered a huge growth in accumulation of property and extent of income,[13] a result of the fact that oil in those countries is state-owned, and revenues from oil export flowed into government — that is, the rulers' — coffers.

Another social group in the oil countries whose accumulated capital and level of income rose considerably was the private business sector. The growth of wealth of this group stemmed from the steep rise in demand for their services, the significant increase in the import of goods, and the encouragement given to private investors to participate in large-scale construction and development projects.[14] The business sector also gained financially from the high inflation rates during the oil decade in the economies under review.

The condition of certain other social groups, however — the civil service, and salaried employees in the private sector — was different. While the real income of most, if not all, of these employees increased — in some cases by 20-25 percent in real terms annually — the gap between these strata on the one hand, and the elite and the upper middle class on the other, widened considerably.[15] There was also a worsening economic situation in some of the bottom levels of the oil societies, where income fell in real terms. A prime example was Iran, where there was a deterioration in the condition of the landless peasantry. As

Figure I.1
Six Arab countries: enrollment rates for the second level of education, 1970, 1975 and 1981-2

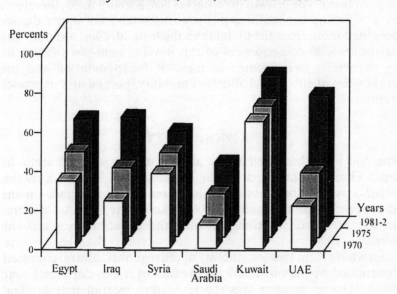

Source: table I.1

9

a result of agrarian reform and the introduction of widespread mechanization in farming, many of the peasants there lost their livelihood and migrated to the big cities, but were unable to find permanent employment there and ended up inhabiting the shantytowns of Tehran, Tabriz and other major cities.[16] Moreover, the governments of many of the oil countries did not implement effective fiscal mechanisms to reduce inequality in the distribution of wealth and income. A tool as important as progressive income tax did not exist at all (e.g., in Saudi Arabia) or was ineffective (e.g., in Iran). The growth in resources was accompanied, therefore, by a widening economic gap. Proportionately, the upper deciles benefited more from the boom than the lower deciles, although the harshest social consequences of this development were mitigated by the rise in real income of most of the population and the opening up of effective channels of mobility, particularly in private business.

POLITICAL ASPECTS

The "oil effect" marked many aspects of the political arena as well. Three important areas to be considered are its leverage, either way, on the stability of local regimes; its impact on the ideology of Arab unity and pan-Arab solidarity; and its influence on the nature of relations between the oil economies and the West.

To what extent was the stability of the regimes in the oil countries determined by the oil effect? On the face of it, developments were polar. At one extreme was the revolution in Iran that brought to power a theocratic regime led by a new political elite of Shi'i clerics. At the other extreme, the Arab oil states enjoyed stability and continuity to a degree unknown since the 1950s, a situation that was characteristic both of regimes that had undergone a military coup d'etat (Iraq, Libya) and of conservative monarchies (Saudi Arabia, Kuwait). One of the causes of this political polarity, relevant because of its association with the oil effect, was the different manner that petrodollars were used in Iran until 1979 as compared with the Arab oil states. In Iran, the manner of the disbursement of the oil revenues aroused opposition and mounting hostility toward Muhammad Riza Shah and his regime, which meant that a powerful lever of state rule — available economic resources — boomeranged. Instead of increasing support for the regime, these resources weakened the regime, owing to several factors. First, the glaringly uneven distribution of resources among the various sectors of the Iranian population provoked anger. The Arab regimes showed greater sensitivity in this respect, realizing the importance of distributing wealth in a way that would appear fair according to the criteria prevalent in their societies. Second, the Shah's massive expenditure on economic development aroused hostility because of its very scope, and what many considered its over-rapid modernization. In the Arab countries, too, heavy investment was made in economic systems, but the rulers proved to be more concerned about social cost. Even so, the Arab oil countries also witnessed developments that raised doubts about the immunity of their regimes to popular resentment. In the case of the monarchical oil states, several scholars have stressed the growing gap between the rising social status and self-awareness of the middle class — in particular its medium and upper strata — and its low political status, that is, the lack of appropriate representation and influence in the foci of political power. This gap continues to harbor a threat to the stability of these regimes.[17]

A significant political development during the oil decade was the decline of the ideal of Arab unity and pan-Arab solidarity. Two events stand out in this connection. The first is the separate peace agreement which Egypt made with Israel in 1979. The state that had led the Arab world since the 1950s in its struggle to realize Arab unity transgressed a basic injunction in the perception of Arab nationalism both ideologically and politically by its very recognition of the neighboring Zionist state, not to mention its willingness to live with it in peace. The second blow was related to the Gulf War between Iraq and Iran, when Iran attained political, economic and military support from Syria and Libya — two of the more radical Arab states in their views of Arab unity and solidarity. The Arab world, therefore, became deeply divided in light of its relations with non-Arab states — Israel and Iran — during the oil decade. The oil factor, of course, was not the sole cause of the crisis that undermined Arab unity, but revenues from oil exacerbated the differences in the economic conditions of the Arab states, particularly between the sparsely inhabited oil states of the Arabian Peninsula and the densely populated countries of the Nile Valley. The yawning gap in available resources for consumption and investment between Saudi Arabia and Kuwait, on the one hand, and Egypt and Sudan on the other, put the concept of unity to a difficult test. The poor Arab states demanded a significant share of the unexpected riches, and when this demand was rejected, the attitude of the poor states toward the meaning and validity of the idea of Arab unity veered away sharply. In the case of Egypt, severe economic and political constraints prompted requests for economic assistance from its wealthy Arab neighbors. When the oil states refused to countenance these demands, Egypt embarked on a new path, no longer consonant with the ideology of Arab nationalism as it had crystallized after the First World War.[18]

The tension between the two Ba'thist regimes — the Syrian and the Iraqi — was also fueled to a considerable extent by the gap in available resources and in the rate of economic development and military aggrandizement between the two states during the first few years following the sharp rise in oil prices. Like Egypt, although in different circumstances, Syria expected and requested a generous share of the oil revenues from its eastern neighbor.[19] Its disappointment at Iraq's refusal to seriously consider these requests was one of the causes of the conflict that developed between them, to the extent of Syria's providing support for Iran in the Gulf War. By the end of the oil decade, the Arab states appeared to have come to terms with the fact that the realization of the vision of Arab unity was more distant than ever. Evidence of pan-Arab solidarity was scarce.

Toward the end of the 1970s, when the dependence of the Western economies on Middle East oil reached its high point and the oil states in the region enjoyed their greatest economic power, it seemed to many leaders of the oil states that the time was ripe to establish a new type of relationship with the West. No longer would it be a relationship between unequal partners, with the West retaining the power to determine the course of economic and political developments, but between sides that were evenly balanced, each with its own strengths and weaknesses and each dependent on the economic welfare and political stability of the other. Oil was deemed to be the compensatory factor in a heretofore unequal system. It followed that in such a new system, the Middle East oil states would have the capacity to bring about (or even impose) a change in the attitudes, postures and decisions of the Western states in areas of importance to the oil states.

Indeed, the change that occurred in official Western attitudes toward the oil states and their rulers during the latter half of the 1970s was remarkable. It was reflected not only in the ceremonial aspect of the relationship but, far more important, in a willingness to supply advanced technology and weaponry to the oil states.

Moreover, there was an actual shift in policy by the Western states in areas where the oil states pressed for change, primarily in their posture toward the Arab-Israeli conflict. In the economic sphere, partnerships between Western companies and Arab firms, both public and private, were established, with Arab financial interests exerting considerable influence on Western money markets.

Ultimately, there was not enough weight in these changes to alter the essential nature of relations between the West and the Middle East oil states. Oil indeed imparted power to these states which they did not possess prior to the price revolution, but a balanced and weighted system of relations was not established. Ironically, by the end of the oil decade, the major oil exporters of the region recognized that their economic dependence on the Western countries had actually grown in comparison with the period before 1973-74. This was evident mainly in dependence on revenues deriving from the major oil consumers, as well as dependence on their supply of goods and technology. There was, of course, no viable alternative to the technology offered by the Western economies and Japan during the decade under review. Moreover, the utilization of Western technology for the construction of the oil states' infrastructure and the establishment of petrochemical industries made the transfer to alternative technologies at a later stage economically unfeasible because of the costs involved. Such dependence was intensified by the high levels of expenditure on consumption and investment that had become customary in the fat years of the oil decade. These levels of spending created a chain of expectations and habits which the elites of the oil states found difficult to break. Under these conditions, Western countries such as Britain and the United States, themselves major oil producers, were able to influence oil prices on the world market and, consequently, affect the revenues of the oil states. In the political arena, the dependence of the regimes in Saudi Arabia, Kuwait and the United Arab Emirates on the United States increased as a result of the political aspirations of both Iran and Iraq.

The increasing economic dependence of the oil states on the West in the years following the oil decade confirms the conclusion that no fundamental change had occurred in relations between the two sides. Ultimately, this greater economic dependence resulted from the response of the oil states, primarily Saudi Arabia, to pressures by the consumer states, particularly the United States, to produce oil in larger quantities than the oil states wished.

13

Compliance with this pressure arose from the weakness of the producers in the face of Western pressure,[20] setting off a chain of developments and processes whose end was deeper economic dependence.

CONCLUSION

In its force and magnitude, the oil factor came as a surprise not only to the consumer states but to the major Opec producers themselves. In the absence of economic master plans to exploit the billions of dollars that flooded the oil countries, economic strategies and plans were formulated simultaneously with the progression of the boom. Expectations of change by the rulers as well as by the populations of the oil states at the beginning of the oil decade were vast, but most of them did not materialize. The first cycle of plenty from the income of oil exports came at a time when the governments and rulers of the oil states were unprepared for it.

It was in the political sphere that change was most circumscribed. An examination of developments related to the stability of the regimes and to inter-Arab and international relations shows that the "oil effect" acted to strengthen the status quo and the conservative forces in the region. In some respects, the Islamic revolution in Iran was also a manifestation of this tendency. Generally, the power of the monarchical Arab regime was enhanced, the status of the separate nation-state was reinforced, and there was a marked improvement in the position of the Western states in the region, with dependence on them increasing.

No radical change took place in economic structure either. No economic revolution could have occurred under the conditions that existed in the oil states, nor could one have occurred in such a relatively short period of time. However, fundamental and far-reaching changes were made in the development of physical infrastructures. Even more significant, in the long run, were the changes that took place on the social plane during the oil decade, namely the settlement of the nomads, the acceleration of urbanization, the rapid expansion of educational systems, especially on the secondary and higher levels, and the growth and cohesion of the social and economic power of the middle class.

Why did the oil states fail to register more impressive achievements in the economic and political spheres? That they themselves were surprised by the extent of their riches is only a partial answer. In the case of the desert oil states, the explanation lies in certain abiding characteristics, principally the stark imbalance between the excess of wealth and the shortage of local manpower. Moreover, the absorption of advanced technologies encountered obstacles in the form of traditional patterns of production. In the case of both Iran and Iraq, the Islamic revolution in the former, and the war between them, harmed extant economic achievements and prevented the implementation of proposed plans. Developments both in the desert countries and in the populated oil states showed that there were no shortcuts to modernization. While the progress that was made must not be belittled, the oil societies were only at the start of the road to the goals they had set for themselves at the beginning of the oil decade.

NOTES

1. Figures based on *PE*, May 1977 p. 167; June 1981, p. 232; and July 1985, p. 236.
2. For figures on GDP (current prices) in 1981, see WB, *World Development Report 1983*, New York: Oxford University Press, 1983, pp. 136–37, table 2 (hereafter: *World Development Report*).
3. *Monthly Petroleum Statistics Reports*, various issues, 1977.
4. See and compare Richard F. Nyprop et al., *Area Handbook for Saudi Arabia*, 3rd ed., Washington, DC: The American University, 1977, p. 67; J.S. Birks, "The Impact of Economic Development on Pastoral Nomadism in the Middle East: An Inevitable Eclipse?" in Howard Bowen-Jones (ed.), *Change and Development in the Middle East*, London: Methuen, 1981, p. 84.
5. *World Development Report 1984*, pp. 260-61, table 22.
6. *Mideast Report*, 15 August 1983. Cf. Nazli Choucri, "Migration in the Middle East: Transformation and Change," *MER 6/2* (1983-84): 17-23; Eliyahu Kanovsky, "Migration from the Poor to the Rich Arab Countries," *Occasional Papers*, no. 85, Tel Aviv University, June 1984, pp. 56-77.
7. See and compare IMF, *International Financial Statistics*, December 1984, July 1985 and July 1986 (hereafter: *International Financial Statistics*); *QER: Egypt*, Annual Supplement 1984; *QER: Jordan*, Annual Supplement 1983; *QER: Syria*, Annual Supplement 1983.
8. SIPRI, *World Armaments and Disarmament Yearbook 1983*, London: Taylor and Francis, 1983, pp. 162-63, table 7A.2.
9. UNIDO, *Handbook of Industrial Statistics*, New York: UNIDO, 1982. *World Development Report 1984*, pp. 222-23, table 3.
10. For data on investments in physical infrastructure, see SAMA, *Annual Report 1399* (1979), Jidda, 1980; UN, *Statistical Yearbook of Asia and the Pacific 1982*, Bangkok: UN, 1982, pp. 234-35, tables 23, 27-28.
11. UNESCO, *SY 1984*, Paris: UN, 1984, pp. IV-6-14, table 4.1.
12. Ibid., pp. III-20-71.
13. See, e.g., *New York Times*, 10 January 1979; *Financial Times*, 29 July 1990.

14. Robert Graham, *Iran: The Illusion of Power*, New York: St. Martin's Press, 1979, pp. 47-49; Rostam M. Kavoussi, "Economic Growth and Income Distribution in Saudi Arabia," *ASQ* 5/1 (1983): 74-78 (hereafter: Kavoussi, "Economic Growth"); 'Isam al-Khafaji, "State Incubation of Iraqi Capitalism," and James Paul, "The New Bourgeoisie of the Gulf," *MERIP Reports*, September-October 1986, pp. 4-9, 18-22.
15. M.H. Pesaran, "Economic Development and Revolutionary Upheavals in Iran," in Haleh Afshar (ed.), *Iran: A Revolution in Turmoil*, Hampshire: Macmillan, 1985, pp. 29-31, 34. For a different view, see N. Momayezi, "Economic Correlates of Political Violence: The Case of Iran," *MEJ* 40 (1986): 71-81.
16. Farhad Kazemi, *Poverty and Revolution in Iran*, New York and London: New York University Press, 1980, pp. 35-42 and *passim*.
17. Mark Heller and Nadav Safran, "The New Middle Class and Regime Stability in Saudi Arabia," *Harvard Middle East Papers* 3 (1985): 7-26 (hereafter: Heller and Safran, "The New Middle Class").
18. See below, pp. 67-69.
19. Amatzia Baram, *National [wataniyya] Integration and Exclusiveness in Political Thought and Practice in Iraq under the Ba'th, 1968-82* (in Hebrew), Ph.D. Thesis (The Hebrew University of Jerusalem, 1986), p. 230.
20. For a detailed discussion of this development, see Abbas Alnasrawi, *Opec in a Changing World Economy*, Baltimore and London: Johns Hopkins University Press, 1985, pp. 112-16.

1

The Struggle for Control

From the outset, oil deposits discovered throughout the Middle East were by law the property of the states in whose territory they were found. Nevertheless, for a period of some 60 years — from the early 1920s until well into the 1970s — a relentless and at times violent struggle was waged over control of the region's oil industry. At first it was the foreign (American and European) oil companies who alone possessed the know-how and capital necessary to produce the oil and transport it to the consumer market. The only way local governments benefited was through the concessions they extended to these companies. This arrangement left the oil companies in full control of production, which meant that they could dictate how much oil to produce, where to market it, and even how much of their profits to remit to the local government or ruler — a situation clearly too good to last for very long. The struggle for control that followed played itself out simultaneously on two levels: (1) between the foreign companies themselves in their competition for concessions, and (2) between the oil companies and the local rulers over shares in profits. By the late 1970s, local governments had secured full control of production and, with it, far-reaching economic and political power.

MAJORS AGAINST MAJORS

The sixty-year struggle for the control of Middle Eastern oil may be said to have passed through five stages. The first spanned the

17

1920s and 1930s, a period of intense competition for the control of production in Iraq among the major oil companies themselves, at first between the British Anglo-Persian Oil Company and British Royal-Dutch Shell, and then between these two companies and the American Majors, principally Standard Oil of New Jersey (SONJ). As far back as the pre-First World War period, it had been widely believed that Iraq was rich in oil, especially in its northern province, the vilayet of Mosul. A concession granted by the Ottoman sultan led to the founding in 1914 of the Turkish Petroleum Company (TPC), controlled by British companies from the start. The Anglo-Persian Oil Company held 50 percent of its shares; the Anglo-Saxon Petroleum Company, which represented Shell, held 25 percent; and the remaining 25 percent was acquired by a German investor, the Deutsche Bank. The collapse of the Ottoman Empire in the First World War, the conquest of Iraq by British forces, and the establishment of the British mandatory regime in Iraq strengthened the control of the British government and British companies over Iraqi oil. The British government expropriated Deutsche Bank's holdings in TPC, which in 1920 were transferred to the French government as part of the San Remo peace conference agreement. The French, accordingly, formed the Compagnie Française des Petrole. TPC was now entirely under British-French control.[1]

These developments were a source of irritation to several of the American oil companies, especially SONJ and Socony–Vacuum, which were eager to expand their production capacity outside the United States and found Iraq's potential most attractive. These companies succeeded in conjuring up, and then exploiting, an atmosphere of concern in the United States over the depletion of American US oil sources and the dependability of the regular supply. They also harnessed the administration and the State Department to their struggle to gain a share of Iraqi oil. The State Department insisted that Britain and France apply the Open Door Policy — non-discrimination in economic activity within the mandated areas — to which they had committed themselves. After drawn-out negotiations, the British government agreed in 1928 to transfer 25 percent of the TPC shares owned by Anglo-Persian to a group of five American oil companies organized as the Near East Development Corporation, dominated by SONJ and Socony–Vacuum. TPC changed its name to IPC (Iraq Petroleum Company) in 1929 and became a production company under joint ownership of British (47.50 percent), American (23.75 percent) and French (23.75 percent) firms. The remaining 5 percent was acquired by an Armenian geologist and businessman, Calouste Gulbenkian ("Mr. Five Percent"), who was rewarded thus for services he had rendered in the establishment of the Turkish-Iraqi oil company.[2]

Until the early 1930s, most areas of production in the Middle East were in the hands of European companies, especially Anglo-Persian, which controlled oil production in Iran exclusively and which, together with Shell, held about half the shares of IPC. The American oil companies had obtained only a relatively small share of Iraqi oil, along with control of the Bahrain Petroleum Company. However, a major change in the status of American involvement in the Middle East oil industry, marking the second stage in the regional struggle for control, was initiated in 1933 when the ruler of Saudi Arabia, 'Abd al-'Aziz Ibn Sa'ud, awarded Socal a concession to produce oil in an area of 728,000 square km in the country's eastern provinces. Socal hurriedly split the ownership of the Saudi concession with another American company, Texaco, in order to actualize the vast oil production potential within the concession area. The two established a joint production company, Caltex (California Texas Oil Company), in 1936, and in 1938 discovered oil in commercial quantities in their concession area. In 1944 they adopted a new name for their production company in Saudi Arabia, Aramco (Arabian American Oil Company).

The growing demand for oil following the Secord World War and the immense production potential in Saudi Arabia prompted the two Aramco partners to invite two other American Majors to join their ranks in 1948, SONJ and Mobil, thereby increasing total investment in the Saudi oil industry and opening up new marketing channels. The four American Majors owned the company jointly, with Socal, Texaco and SONJ holding 30 percent of the shares each, and Mobil holding 10 percent. Within less than two decades, Aramco had become the biggest oil producing company in the world and Saudi Arabia the largest oil exporter in the Middle East and one of the three largest exporting states in the world, together with the United States and the Soviet Union.

It may seem curious that Saudi oil came to be controlled entirely by American companies at a time when Britain enjoyed undisputed control in the Persian Gulf area and considerable influence among the rulers of Saudi Arabia, and when European oil companies still controlled most of the concessions and most of the production in the region. Significantly, while an intense

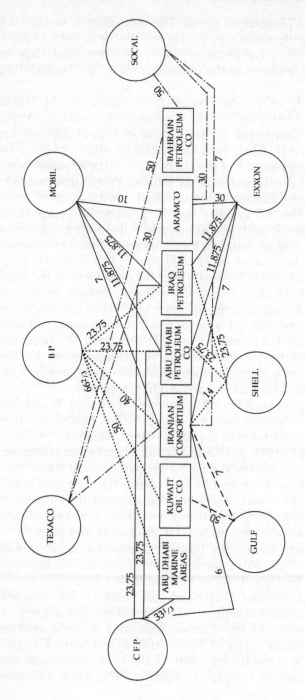

Illustration 1.1
Ownership links (in %): Majors and the main oil producing companies in the Middle East, 1954

and prolonged struggle had been waged over control of the Iraqi oil concession, the American companies did not have to exert themselves in order to win the Saudi oil concession. In contrast to TPC, Saudi Arabia dropped into American hands like a ripe plum.

The reason for this lies in the production and marketing capacity of the European oil companies, particularly of Anglo-Persian and Shell. These companies handled a vast amount of crude oil that they produced in the Middle East and in other parts of the world, and their share of the world market did not allow them to significantly expand production further. Since they were not inclined to develop new oil fields, they were not intent on winning the Saudi Arabian concession. Furthermore, their geologists reported that the chances of finding substantial commercial quantities of oil in eastern Saudi Arabia were slight. Although when Socal discovered oil in neighboring Bahrain in 1932 the European companies did compete for the Saudi concession, they did not invest very much effort in winning it, whereupon Socal, offering a more enticing financial arrangement to Ibn Sa'ud, acquired the concession.[3]

One of the relevant factors in the unfolding of the Saudi chapter was the nature of the original accord forged between the partners in TPC, known as the "Red Line Agreement." When TPC was created in 1914 the founding companies agreed on a "self-denying" clause, whereby they undertook not to produce oil in Ottoman Empire territory outside the framework of the Turkish Petroleum Company. This clause, which was retained in the 1928 agreement with the group of American companies that joined TPC as well, and which was carried over when TPC became IPC, became known as the Red Line Agreement because of a red line that was drawn on the appended map around the former Asian and European domains of the Ottoman Empire — Turkey, the Fertile Crescent countries and the Arabian Peninsula, excluding Kuwait (see illustration 1.2). The TPC partners were expected to observe the self-denying clause in these areas. This was a "limiting agreement" in that it greatly circumscribed freedom of action and frustrated initiatives made by some of the individual IPC companies, particularly Gulf, which tried to win production concessions in Bahrain and later in Saudi Arabia. However, the agreement did not prevent the European companies from seeking concessions within the area of the Red Line under the umbrella of IPC, although their attempts in Saudi

Illustration 1.2
The Red Line Agreement, 1928

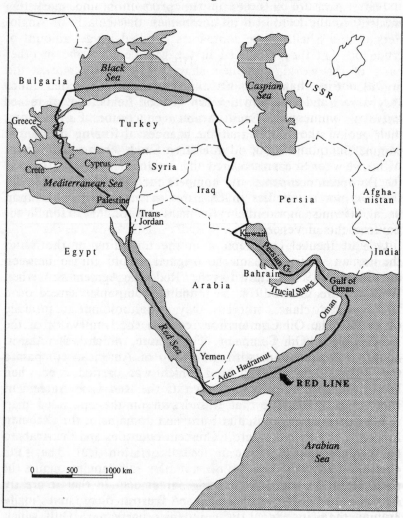

Source: US, National Archives, RG 80, file 30–1–30

Arabia were half-hearted. When IPC did submit a bid to acquire the Saudi concession in 1933, its purpose was more to block other companies than to develop new oil fields. In the long term, the Red Line Agreement did not prevent the two American partners in IPC, New Jersey and Mobil, from moving into the Saudi oil industry: pressure by these companies to join Aramco eventually led to the annulment of the agreement in 1948.[5]

IRAN AGAINST THE MAJORS

It was not by chance that shortly after the long conflict among the Majors had died down, a new contest for control of the oil industry commenced — this time between a domestic government and one of the Majors, although indirectly involving all the Majors operating in the Middle East. In 1949 the government of Iran approved a proposal by the Anglo-Iranian Oil Company (the new name adopted by Anglo-Persian in 1935) to increase the company's royalties to the government on the same basis as agreements signed that year between the Majors and the governments of Venezuela and Saudi Arabia, known as the "fifty-fifty" agreements.[6] The proposal, however, required ratification by the Iranian Majlis (parliament). A special Majlis Oil Commission appointed in 1950 decided to reject the oil agreement altogether. After months of debate in the Majlis, a consensus emerged on Iran's need to take control of its natural resources, especially of its oil. The Oil Commission recommended in 1951 that the Anglo-Iranian Oil Company be nationalized, and the Majlis, adopting the recommendation by a decisive majority, passed the Nationalization Law. Simultaneously, the politician who had been the driving force behind the nationalization movement, Dr. Muhammad Mussadeq, was elected prime minister.

Mussadeq threw himself into the task of implementing the new law with fervor. All Anglo-Iranian installations were earmarked to be requisitioned by the newly founded National Iranian Oil Company (NIOC). The British company did not recognize the nationalization law as valid, and a bitter dispute was carried on between the Iranian government on the one hand, and Anglo-Iranian, the British government and the other Majors on the other. This conflict lasted until the military coup of August 1953 which toppled the Mussadeq government and relegated the political forces that had backed it to the sidelines for a whole generation.

The Iranian attempt at nationalization came to naught, and

production of Iranian oil was to remain under the control of foreign companies for many years. The reason for this failure was that the Iranian government could not market the oil that the NIOC produced. This led to a steep fall in foreign currency revenues and a large deficit in balance of payments. Iran soon faced a serious economic crisis, which Mussadeq's regime was unable to handle.

The inability of NIOC to export oil reflected the conditions that prevailed in the world oil industry in the early 1950s. First, the oil shortfall on the world market resulting from Iran's efforts at nationalization was easily redressed by other sources. Some of the producing countries had an unexploited production capacity, and the oil-exporting governments were generally eager to increase production in their territory. The oil states in the Middle East and elsewhere, far from demonstrating solidarity with the Iranian government during its conflict with the oil companies, took advantage of the opportunity to increase production of their own. Secondly, the Majors backed Anglo-Iranian, aware that the struggle of the British company against the nationalization law was also very much their own. If the attempt to nationalize oil succeeded in Iran, it would be repeated in other oil-producing countries in the Middle East and elsewhere throughout the world. This was a struggle for survival, and the Majors fought with all their might. They still controlled most of the means of transporting and refining oil (the "downstream" industries in the 1950s), which enabled them to block the marketing of Iranian oil. They also threatened legal and economic action against any purchaser of Iranian oil, claiming that the oil had been seized illegally by the Iranian government. The embargo, which was almost total, worked. The gaps in it were too insignificant to enable Mussadeq's government to survive economically.[7]

The arrangement that eventually settled the oil dispute in Iran, which came into force in 1954, involved the formation of a consortium of foreign oil companies known as Iran Oil Participants (IOP), which replaced the Anglo-Iranian Oil Company. The consortium consisted of Anglo-Iranian, whose name was changed to BP (British Petroleum), holding 40 percent of the consortium shares; Shell, with 14 percent; the American Majors, with 7 percent each; the Compagnie Française des Petrole, with 6 percent; and a group of six American Independents organized as Iricon Agency, with 5 percent. The chief consequence of the Iranian attempt to nationalize, then, was the loss of exclusive control by the Anglo-

24

Iranian Oil Company and the acquisition of a share in Iran's oil production by all the Majors, both European and American, as well as by a group of Independents. The consortium made a single gesture to the Iranian government: the transfer of the Naft-i Shah oil field and the Kermanshah refinery to the control of NIOC.[8]

The failure of Iran's nationalization attempt had other consequences as well, both domestic and international. The years of struggle left a residue of bitter resentment in Iran. Anger at the Western companies and at the governments of Britain and the United States, which had prevented Iran from actualizing its right to control and benefit from its own natural resource after years of prolonged political and economic crises, was widespread among broad segments of society. Many Iranians never forgave the Shah, who instead of supporting nationalization became a puppet of the Western powers. These sentiments were harbored for a quarter of a century after the nationalization episode, exploding in full fury in the Islamic revolution: Khomeyni was to harvest what Mussadeq had sown but failed to reap. Outside Iran the lesson of the failure of nationalization and the heavy price it exacted was learned well. Not a single oil state attempted nationalization of the oil industry in its territory during the rest of the 1950s or the 1960s. Even at the peak of their power in the 1970s most of the large oil exporters shunned any unilateral move toward nationalization, with the exception of Libya and Iraq.

MAJORS AGAINST NON-MAJORS

Changing market conditions, however, would achieve what political action could not, a phenomenon that became evident in the latter 1950s and again in the early 1970s, marking the fourth stage in the struggle for control of oil production. The sizable increase in oil consumption in industrialized economies that lacked abundant energy resources, such as Italy and Japan, forced them to seek ways of reducing their dependency on the Majors, which were their chief oil suppliers, and thereby reduce rising outlays in foreign currency on oil imports. In 1953 the Italian government formed a public holding company, ENI, comprising all public oil and gas companies in Italy. ENI also set up an exploration and production company operating outside Italy, AGIP (Azienda General Italiana Petrol), which made vigorous efforts to win production concessions in the Middle East. However, its attempts to acquire holding shares in the IOP consortium companies failed.

The Majors, which had been forced to succumb to pressure by the US Administration and Congress and grant holding shares to the group of Independents, did not feel compelled to respont in a similar way to AGIP's pleas for a share of Iranian oil. ENI's director, Enrico Mattei, then set himself the task of breaking the nearly absolute control by the Majors over Middle East oil production, first by seeking to acquire production rights in areas outside the concessions controlled by the Majors. In order to persuade local governments to grant concessions to a newcomer like AGIP, Mattei proposed, inter alia, that the new agreements be based on cooperation in control of production between the foreign company and the domestic oil company. The first agreement of this kind was signed between AGIP and the Egyptian government in 1957. An even more important agreement was signed that year between AGIP and the NIOC,[9] formulating the principle of shared control in a joint production company, Sirip, which began to produce oil in the northern waters of the Persian Gulf in 1960.

The outcome of the ENI agreements was that the principle of joint control became the cornerstone of all new accords between foreign and national oil production companies in the Middle East. For example, shared control lay at the foundation of the concessions that the Iranian government granted in 1958 to Standard Oil Company (Indiana), an Independent American company, and the concessions that the Saudi and Kuwaiti governments granted in 1957-58 to the Japan Petroleum Trading Company.[10] These agreements conflicted with what the Majors regarded as the optimal format of the relationship between the foreign production company and the domestic government. In fact, the signing of the agreements, as well as the expansion of operations by non-Majors — American, European and Japanese oil companies — in the joint venture framework presaged the end of the era of exclusive control by foreign companies over oil production. Moreover, these developments also eroded the status of the Majors in their negotiations with the local governments over both old and new concessions. The emergence of the joint venture framework thus contributed to the reversal that took place in the control of oil production in the Middle East at the start of the 1970s.

OPEC IN CONTROL

The fifth stage in the struggle for control took place during 1971-79, when the Majors lost control of oil production in areas where they had enjoyed exclusive rights since the 1920s and 1930s, with control of production passing to domestic national companies. In the early 1970s both Libya and Iraq unilaterally nationalized production concessions and rights that had been granted to foreign companies. Libya nationalized the controlling rights of British Petroleum in 1971, and of Banker Hunt, Shell, Socal and Texaco in 1973 and 1974. Iraq nationalized IPC and its subsidiaries in 1972, 1973 and 1975.[11]

The other oil-producing states in the Middle East avoided unilateral nationalization of the foreign companies, bringing production in their areas under their complete control through an exhaustive sequence of negotiations that lasted throughout most of the 1970s and was called the "participation" process. This process was initiated at the 24th Opec congress, held in 1971, when a resolution was adopted calling on all members of the organization to take immediate steps to apply the principle of participation in the oil production industry.[12] At the beginning of 1972 all the Majors agreed to promote the application of this principle, which meant the transfer of 20 percent of the holding shares of the production companies, such as Aramco and the Kuwait Oil Company, to the national companies. From the moment the Majors accepted the principle of transfer of control, it was merely a matter of time until most or all of the controlling shares passed from the foreign companies to the national companies. The bargaining power of the local governments in the process of transfer of control was further enhanced in October 1973 when Opec began fixing the posted prices of oil on the world market without prior negotiation with the Majors. Within several years, control of the oil that Aramco produced and the facilities belonging to the company passed into the hands of the Saudi government, in two stages: 25 percent control in 1973, and 60 percent control in 1976. Similarly, the shares controlling production in Kuwait were transferred to its national oil company in 1975; in Qatar this occurred in 1976; and in Bahrain it occurred in 1979.[13] The Iranian government was not a party to the "participation" arrangement. In May 1973 it signed an agreement with the consortium of IOP companies affirming that NIOC held all the controlling rights over production of Iranian oil. In return, the consortium companies received an offer to

27

supply NIOC with technical assistance in operating the industry, and were also assured priority in purchasing crude oil from the national company.[14]

By the late 1970s, control of oil production in the concession areas that had been granted to the major oil companies in the early part of the century had passed into the hands of the local governments. The foreign production companies became subcontractors in several of the oil economies, providing technical and administrative services. In certain oil states they had priority over other foreign companies or governments in the purchase of crude oil, and continued as important marketers of local oil. These were the last remnants of their once-formidable status in the oil countries of the Middle East.

The success of the oil-state governments in the 1970s where the Iranian government had failed two decades before was the outcome of a change in several basic conditions of the world oil industry. First, a situation of over-demand prevailed in the world market during most of the 1970s, which meant that the capacity for unexploited production in the short and medium term was reduced. Had there been a fall in production and export from any of the countries in the region as a result of confrontation with the local government, the foreign oil companies could not have supplied the shortage of crude oil from alternative sources. The fact that disruptions in production, which did, in fact, occur in the winter of 1973, could cause tremors in the world oil market greatly enhanced the local government's bargaining power with the Majors, and all the more so with the other companies.

Secondly, the oil industry was incomparably more complex and multi-faceted in the 1970s than it had been in the early 1950s. A large number of new companies had entered this industry. The Majors, therefore, lost their oligopolistic status in the world market. Their share in refining, apart from the United States and the Communist bloc, fell from 73 percent in 1953 to 49 percent in 1972, and their share in marketing distillates decreased in the same period from 72 percent to 54 percent.[15] Furthermore, their share in concession areas shrank from 64 percent to only 24 percent. While the reduction in their share of world production (excluding the United States, the Soviet Union, China and the East European countries) was moderate, from 87 percent to 71 percent, it was sufficient to amount to a loss of control in this area as well.[16] As a result, the Majors no longer had the power to prevent a local government that had resolved to nationalize the foreign companies operating in its territory from marketing the oil the company produced. Thus, British Petroleum, which had fought tenaciously against nationalization in Iran, came to terms over nationalization with the Libyan and the Iraqi governments in 1971 and 1972 respectively.

A third factor that had not existted in the 1950s, and that affected the power balance between the local governments and the Majors, was Opec. The "participation" principle negotiations over the transfer of control were conducted under the auspices of Opec. Moreover, decisions by individual members of the organization to nationalize oil production in their territory were backed by the rest of the members — a markedly different policy from that in the 1950s, when the oil-producing states exploited Iran's aborted marketing to increase their share in the world market.

By the time the sixty-year struggle for control of production in the Middle East ended in the 1970s, not only had the local governments and rulers acquired total oil production revenues for their treasuries, but their control over production provided them with a weapon of enormous political power at home and abroad. Local governments could determine production volume, which in the case of the major producers affected the prices of crude oil on the world market. Control of production also allowed the local governments to decide the destinations of the oil marketed from their territories, albeit with varying degrees of effectiveness. A new form of agreement evolved between producer and consumer governments in the late 1970s onward, for example between Iraq and France, Iran and Japan, and Libya and Turkey.[17]

So long as the oil market experienced conditions of over-demand and was a sellers' market, as in the 1970s, the ability to determine the amount of oil produced, influence prices, fix marketing destinations and dictate terms of supply all imparted political power to the oil-state governments. But this political leverage became greatly attenuated when oversupply conditions — a buyers' market — began to prevail, from 1983 until the end of the decade. In these circumstances the producer governments no longer had the freedom of maneuver to fix supply destinations and conditions of sale. "All buyers are welcome" became the axiom in the oil market after 1983. Still, even in these conditions, control over production was an important asset, not limited to determining prices. Control over production made it possible for domestic governments to devise a long-term oil policy that took into account the volume of proven reserves and the needs of the economy as a whole, apart from the oil industry.

Although they had lost their economic and political power in the Middle East, the Majors found ways of sustaining the high level of profits from their operations in the oil industry. The attitude in the West toward these companies also changed somewhat. After a long period in which politicians, economists and large sectors of the public censured the concentration of such enormous economic power in the hands of a small group of private economic bodies, a revisionist view emerged in the 1980s which held that these companies had acted as a stabilizing factor for a period of decades in a highly complex system. According to this view, low and stable oil prices up until the 1970s had constituted one of the major contributing factors toward the creation of the affluent society in the West in the generation following the Second World War.

NOTES

1. Marian Kent, *Oil and Empire, British Policy and Mesopotamian Oil 1900-1920*, London: Macmillan Press, 1976, pp. 103-12, 137-55; Helmut Mejcher, *Imperial Quest for Oil: Iraq 1910-1928*, London: Ithaca Press, 1976, pp. 110–12 (hereafter: Mejcher).
2. Stephen J. Randall, *United States Foreign Oil Policy, 1919-1948*, Kingston and Montreal: McGill-Queen's University Press, 1985, pp. 33-40; Mejcher, pp. 159–65.
3. Edward Peter Fitzgerald, "The Iraq Petroleum Company, Standard Oil of California, and the Contest for Eastern Arabia, 1930-1933," *IHR* 27 (1991): 331-65.
4. Benjamin Shwadran, *The Middle East, Oil and the Great Powers*, 3rd. ed., New York: John Wiley, 1973, pp. 237–38 (hereafter: Shwadran).
5. Irvine H. Anderson, *Aramco, the United States and Saudi Arabia*, Princeton: Princeton University Press, 1981, pp. 144-59.
6. Zuhayr Mikdashi, *A Financial Analysis of Middle Eastern Oil Concessions: 1901-65*, Praeger: New York, 1966, pp. 135-45, 148-51.
7. Homa Katouzian, *The Political Economy of Modern Iran*, New York and London: New York University Press, 1981, pp. 164-87; Farhad Diba, *Mohammad Mossadeq*, London: Croom Helm, 1986, pp. 95-146.
8. *OPEC, Selected Documents of the International Petroleum Industry. Iran. Pre-1966*, Vienna: Information Department of *OPEC*, 1972, pp. 7-56.
9. Ibid., pp. 67-100.
10. Shwadran, pp. 164, 374.
11. M.K. Nawaz, "Nationalization of Foreign Oil Companies — Libyan Decree of 1 September 1973," *IJIL* 14 (1984): 7-80; Iraq Petroleum Company, *Review for 1972*, London, 1973.
12. Pierre Terzian, *OPEC: The Inside Story*, London: Zed Books, 1985, p. 151.
13. Ian Skeet, *Opec: Twenty-Five Years of Prices and Politics*, Cambridge: Cambridge University Press, 1988, pp. 75-78, 109, 116 (hereafter: Skeet); Shukri M. Ghanem, *OPEC: The Rise and Fall of an Exclusive Club*, London: KPI, 1986, pp. 158-60.

15. Neil H. Jacoby, *Multinational Oil: A Study in Industrial Dynamics*, New York: Macmillan, 1974, p. 211, table 9.12.
16. Ibid.
17. Ian M. Torrens, *Changing Structures in the World Oil Market*, Paris: The Atlantic Institute for International Affairs, 1980, 26-28.

2

The Economics of Interdependence:
The United States and the Arab World, 1973-77

Highly developed economies in the twentieth century have seldom been seen to depend for their growth rates or their degree of stability and affluence on economies that only recently embarked on the road to economic modernization. The United States, for one, never knew such a dependence during most of its economic history. That is, until the late 1960s, which brought the first signs of a growing dependency by the American economy on a number of Middle Eastern and North African oil economies. This trend was to become manifest in the early years of the oil decade. Conversely, the way Arab economies in general and Arab oil states in particular developed resulted in an ever-growing dependency on the United States. The period from 1973 through 1977 marked the beginning of this interdependence.

ECONOMIC DEPENDENCE OF THE UNITED STATES
ON THE ARAB STATES[1]

At the root of the economic dependence of the United States on the Arab world lay the ever-increasing importation of oil. In a matter of a few years, the proportion of oil imported from members of the Organization of Arab Petroleum Exporting Countries (OAPEC) out of total American oil consumption (crude and refined products) rose sharply, from 5 percent in 1972 to 20 percent in 1977, while the proportion of OAPEC oil out of total oil imports into the United States rose from 17 percent in 1972 to 43 percent in 1977 (see table 2.1). By mid-1977, the OAPEC states

Table 2.1

*US consumption and imports of crude oil
and refined products, 1970-77*

(millions of barrels per day and percentage)

	1970	1971	1972	1973	1974	1975	1976	1977
Total consumption	14.6	15.1	16.2	17.4	16.6	16.3	17.4	19.1
Total imports	3.4	3.9	4.7	6.3	6.1	6.0	7.3	8.9
Imports from OAPEC	0.3	0.4	0.8	1.4	1.3	1.8	2.8	3.8
Imports from OAPEC as % of consumption	2	3	5	8	8	11	16	20
Imports from OAPEC as % of total imports	9	10	17	22	21	30	38	43

Source:
US, Department of Energy, *Monthly Petroleum Statistics Reports*, 1977.

were supplying almost half the quantity of crude oil imported into the United States (see table 2.2). Three Arab oil exporters contributed to this development: Saudia Arabia, first and foremost (about 19 percent of total oil imports to the United States in 1976), Libya (7 percent) and Algeria (6 percent; see table 2.3). In 1976 Saudi Arabia was the largest oil supplier to the United States, taking precedence over Venezuela, Nigeria and Canada (see table 2.4).

The reasons for this rapid development in the American oil market were: (1) annual growth rates of consumption outstripping growth rates of oil production in the United States itself; (2) a dwindling of proven reserves, while the quantity of oil produced annually in Venezuela, which had been the largest traditional oil supplier of the United States, declined; and (3) an increase in proven reserves, real production capacity and quantity actually produced in a number of Arab oil states.

The increase, in absolute terms, in the import of OAPEC oil to the United States, from 0.8 million barrels a day in 1972 to 3.8 million barrels a day in 1977, together with the sharp rises in the price of crude oil on the world market in October 1973 and again in January 1974, led to a steep increase in American expenditure for the import of this oil. Payments to the OAPEC economies, totaling some $0.6 billion in 1972, jumped to about $16.5 billion in 1977 (current prices).[2] This development gave rise

33

Table 2.2
US imports of crude oil from OAPEC, 1973-76

	September 1973[a]		1974 average		1975 average		1976 average	
	'000 b/d	%	'000 b/d	%	'000 b/d	%	'000 b/d	%
Algeria	124	3.6	180	5.2	264	6.4	408	7.7
Egypt	—	—	9	0.3	5	0.1	17	0.3
Iraq	17	0.5	—	—	2	..	26	0.5
Kuwait	44	1.3	5	0.1	4	0.1	1	i
Libya	153	4.4	4	0.1	223	5.4	444	8.4
Qatar	41	1.2	17	0.5	18	0.4	24	0.5
Saudi Arabia	599	17.3	438	12.6	701	17.1	1,222	23.1
United Arab Emirates	88	2.5	69	2.0	117	2.9	255	4.8
Total OAPEC	1,066	30.7[b]	722	20.8	1,334	32.5[b]	2,397	24.3
Total imports	3,471	100.0	3,477	100.0	4,105	100.0	5,287	100.0

Notes:
a Pre-crisis level (prior to the oil embargo).
b Components do not add up to totals because of rounding.

Source:
US, Department of Energy, *Monthly Petroleum Statistics Reports, 1977.*

Table 2.3
US imports of crude oil and refined products
from OAPEC, 1975-76
(estimates)

	1975		1976	
	'000 b/d	%	'000 b/d	%
Algeria	290	4.8	437	6.0
Iraq	10	0.2	38	0.5
Kuwait	30	0.5	9	0.1
Libya	330	5.5	532	7.3
Saudi Arabia	850	14.1	1,371	18.8
United Arab Emirates	170	2.8	319	4.4
Others[a]	90	1.5	90	1.2
Total OAPEC	1,770	29.4	2,796	38.3
Total imports	6,030	100.0	7,295	100.0

Note:

a Including Bahrain, Egypt, Qatar and Syria.

Source:

US, Department of Energy, 1977.

Table 2.4
Eight leading oil exporters (crude and refined products)
to the US, 1975-76
(estimates)

	1975		1976	
	'000 b/d	%	'000 b/d	%
Venezuela	1,040	17.2	985	13.5
Saudi Arabia	850	14.1	1,371	18.8
Nigeria	820	13.6	1,124	15.4
Canada	800	13.3	599	8.2
Iran	500	8.3	548	7.5
Indonesia	450	7.5	573	7.8
Libya	330	5.5	532	7.3
Algeria	290	4.8	437	6.0
Total eight exporters	5,080	84.2	6,169	84.6
Total US imports	6,030	100.0	7,295	100.0

Source:

US, Department of Energy, 1977.

to a chain reaction comprising efforts to bring about an increase in American visible exports to the Arab oil economies, an increase in American income from the supply of services to the OAPEC economies, and a rise in the nominal and real value of Arab assets in the American economy.

The greatly increased volume of Arab oil imported into the United States between 1973 and 1977 brought about a profound change in America's balance of trade with the Arab economies. The proportion of America's visible imports accounted for by Arab economies rose from 1 percent in 1972 to over 11 percent in 1977. Since this leap was due solely to the increase in oil imports and the rise in the price of oil, both the federal administration and various private firms were spurred to take steps to increase exports to the OAPEC economies. Simultaneously, in 1974 and 1975 the oil countries embarked on large-scale development plans, the most wide-ranging and ambitious of which was the Saudi Arabian five-year plan (1975-80). These plans opened up new trade possibilities, and explain the increase in American visible exports to the Arab states from $1.2 billion in 1972 to $7.1 billion in 1976 and $8.2 billion in 1977 (current prices). Worldwide, the proportion of American visible exports increased in those years from some 2.5 percent to some 7.0 percent (see table 2.5).

The breakdown of American visible exports by destination shows that throughout the period under review, Saudi Arabia maintained its position as the largest consumer in the Arab world of American-made goods. American exports to Saudi Arabia rose significantly, from $0.3 billion in 1972 to $2.8 billion in 1976 and $3.5 billion in 1977 (current prices), while the relative share of American visible exports to Saudi Arabia out of total American visible exports rose from 0.6 percent to 2.9 percent during the 1972–77 period. Kuwait, which in 1972 was the second-largest consumer in the Arab world of American manufactured goods, was superseded in the mid-1970s by Egypt. In 1977 Egypt imported goods from the United States with a total value of over $1.0 billion, a development that followed the considerable increase in economic aid rendered by the United States to Egypt during 1975–77.[3]

The breakdown of American visible exports to the Arab states by product shows that the major portion of the exports, some 74 percent in 1976, consisted of finished industrial products, while the second-largest category, some 17 percent, was foodstuffs (see table 2.6).

Table 2.5
US visible trade with Arab countries, 1972-77
(millions of dollars)

	IMPORTS						EXPORTS					
	1972	1973	1974	1975	1976	1977	1972	1973	1974	1975	1976	1977
Algeria	104.4	215.1	1,090.6	1,358.6	2,343.7	3,064.5	97.7	160.5	315.1	631.8	487.0	526.5
Babrain	20.0	16.6	60.7	100.4	33.1	74.4	26.5	41.4	79.7	90.2	279.5	203.3
Egypt	16.9	25.9	69.8	27.5	111.0	170.0	76.1	225.4	455.2	682.7	810.0	982.4
Iraq	9.5	15.8	0.9	19.1	123.2	381.5	23.3	55.9	284.7	309.7	381.8	210.9
Jordan	0.3	0.3	0.2	0.8	1.5	3.2	65.2	79.4	105.2	195.4	234.0	301.8
Kuwait	49.0	64.9	13.4	111.4	41.1	214.5	111.3	119.5	208.5	366.1	471.5	547.8
Lebanon	20.6	32.7	29.9	33.3	4.9	42.5	130.2	161.6	286.9	402.3	48.5	123.8
Libya	116.2	215.8	1.4	1,044.6	2,406.2	3,796.1	85.1	103.7	139.4	231.5	276.6	313.7
Morocco	11.4	13.7	19.7	10.2	18.4	21.0	57.8	112.9	184.0	199.5	297.0	371.6
Oman	2.8	24.0	20.8	52.7	251.1	424.3	6.6	9.1	36.5	74.7	57.1	56.9
Qatar	5.3	13.3	79.6	56.5	132.7	292.2	13.5	18.8	33.6	50.3	78.7	113.1
Saudi Arabia	193.6	514.5	1,671.2	2,623.3	5,846.8	6,358.5	314.2	441.9	835.2	1,501.8	2,774.1	3,575.3
Sudan	12.2	8.8	26.8	8.1	24.2	19.0	18.2	38.5	64.3	102.6	105.7	87.1
Syria	2.9	5.8	2.1	7.0	10.3	16.2	19.7	20.7	39.6	127.8	272.2	133.6
Tunisia	8.3	32.6	21.4	26.0	59.2	11.2	54.6	60.2	86.9	90.8	82.4	111.3
UAR	26.9	67.2	366.3	682.3	1,531.7	1,640.8	69.2	121.1	229.7	371.5	424.8	515.1
Yemen, AR	0.2	0.2	0.6	0.2	0.3	0.6	2.2	9.6	1.5	8.3	25.4	46.4
Yemen, PDR	2.7	3.8	5.0	0.6	0.8	2.8	0.9	2.6	12.3	2.8	4.4	30.9
Arab countries total	603.2	1,271.0	3,480.4	6,162.6	12,940.2	16,533.3	1,172.3	1,872.8	3,398.3	5,439.8	7,109.9	8,251.5
World total	55,555.2	69,475.7	100,972.3	96,940.3	120,677.4	146,816.7	49,675.7	71,338.8	98,506.3	107,651.8	114,807.1	120,163.2
Arab countries as % of world	1.1	1.8	3.4	6.4	10.7	11.3	2.4	2.5	3.4	5.0	6.2	6.9

Source:
US, Department of Commerce, 1978.

37

Table 2.6

US visible exports by main commodity groups to Arab countries, 1976 (million of dollars)

	Food and animals	Beverages and tobacco	Crude materials[a]	Mineral fuels[b]	Animal and vegetable oils and fats	Chemicals	Manufactured goods	Machinery and transport equipment	Miscellaneous manufactured goods	Unclassified items
Algeria	94.4	0.6	1.1	0.4	16.7	9.6	62.0	288.4	5.7	0.7
Bahrain	4.9	4.4	0.2	6.3	0.3	4.8	10.8	235.2	6.3	5.6
Egypt	304.8	22.4	18.5	18.4	133.1	17.0	46.0	230.6	13.9	2.9
Iraq	54.1	2.2	2.9	0.9	4.9	6.7	10.9	287.1	8.1	3.0
Jordan	26.3	1.5	1.2	2.7	0.7	3.6	10.2	77.5	5.1	3.2
Kuwait	11.7	18.5	0.9	3.3	1.3	7.6	38.1	349.0	29.0	2.9
Lebanon	15.2	5.9	3.9	—	1.1	1.4	2.8	16.4	1.1	0.4
Libya	5.9	7.4	2.9	0.5	—	7.3	18.6	201.3	16.1	6.3
Morocco	93.9	5.0	8.5	0.2	9.5	2.9	9.0	117.1	2.8	1.5
Oman	1.0	0.6	0.1	—	—	1.6	3.4	40.4	2.7	1.1
Qatar	1.4	0.4	0.5	0.2	—	2.9	5.9	62.6	3.4	0.9
Saudi Arabia	153.3	21.8	13.3	18.9	10.1	44.9	303.9	1,881.0	134.1	23.7
Sudan	24.5	0.1	0.2	0.2	1.1	4.9	4.1	68.1	1.5	1.1
Syria	18.2	35.7	1.6	0.1	2.9	3.8	14.3	189.9	3.7	1.9
Tunisia	15.5	0.5	4.6	—	1.9	2.5	2.1	52.2	1.6	0.5
UAR	11.1	14.4	3.2	1.7	0.6	20.7	56.8	291.6	16.7	4.7
Yemen, AR	14.1	—	0.2	—	0.4	0.2	1.2	8.8	0.3	0.3
Yemen, PDR	1.2	—	—	—	0.3	0.1	0.2	1.7	—	0.1
Arab countries total	851.6	141.7	64.0	53.9	185.0	142.2	600.3	4,398.7	252.1	60.8
World total	15,709.7	1,523.3	10,891.4	4,226.1	978.1	9,958.1	11,204.8	49,509.9	6,572.2	2,749.4
Arab countries as % of world	5.4	9.3	0.6	1.3	18.9	1.4	5.4	8.9	3.8	2.2

Notes: a Excluding fuels.
         b Including lubricants.

Source: US, Department of Commerce, 1977.

38

A radical change thus took place in the American balance of trade with the Arab economies. To be sure, both imports and exports grew considerably in both absolute and relative terms, but the annual growth rates of imports were higher than those of exports. Whereas imports in 1972–77 increased 27.5 times, exports increased only 7.0 times. The lower annual growth of exports is explained by the limited capacity for the absorption of industrial products on the part of most Arab oil economies, as well as by the stiff competition from manufacturers from other industrialized countries in the West and from Japan.[4] The outcome of this was that the United States, which until 1973 had enjoyed a surplus in its balance of trade with the Arab states, began suffering a growing deficit in its trade with these countries. During 1976 and 1977 American visible imports surplus in trade with the Arab economies totaled $5.8 billion and $8.5 billion respectively, and the rate of visible imports surplus out of total visible imports from the Arab countries in 1977 reached some 51 percent. This increase, in absolute terms, in the trade deficit with the Arab states contributed significantly to the deficit in the overall United States balance of trade, which totaled $14.6 billion in 1976 and some $27 billion in 1977.

American invisible imports from and exports to the Arab economies also reached considerable proportions during this period. The most important of the invisible import items were payments on account of interest and profits deriving from assets in the United States of the Arab oil states (in both the public and private sectors), especially of Saudi assets.[5] The estimated expenditure of the American economy under this heading during 1974–77 was some $12 billion.[6] Two main items constituted the invisible exports side: net profit of the American oil companies in the Arab states,[7] and net profit of American construction and engineering companies,[8] which in 1975 and 1976 were awarded comprehensive contracts for the execution of projects, mostly in the oil states of the Arabian Peninsula, whose outlay was estimated at some $19 billion.[9] My estimate regarding the aggregate net income of the United States economy during 1974–76 from these two sources totals some $16–17 billion.[10] In the absence of data on the other invisible trade items, it cannot be determined whether on that account too the United States developed a deficit in its commerce with the Arab economies, in contrast to a considreable surplus recorded previously. At the same time, it may be reasonably assumed that even if the United States had a surplus in its balance of invisible trade, this surplus would not have been sufficient to offset the deficit in the balance of trade and to maintain a balanced current account with the Arab economies.

Similarly, a considerable change took place during this period in the sphere of economic aid and unilateral transfers from the United States to the Arab economies. After a long period of aid (grants, loans and technical assistance) provided only on a limited scale, the administration in Washington began pouring large-scale aid into a number of Arab economies. Total American aid approved for the Arab states rose from $127 million in the 1973 fiscal year to about $1.4 billion in the 1978 fiscal year, with total aid approved during the 1974–78 fiscal years reaching some $5.5 billion. Most of the aid went to Egypt ($3.2 billion, representing 59 percent of total aid to the Arab world) and to Jordan ($1.0 billion, representing 19 percent of total aid). Other Arab states receiving aid from the United States were Syria, Lebanon, Sudan, Morocco, Tunisia, North Yemen, Bahrain and Libya. Eighty percent of the total aid to the Arab economies was given in the form of grants and long-term loans to finance projects in the civilian sector, foodstuff import and development projects, as well as to cover deficits in the current accounts of the recipient economies (see table 2.7).

Unilateral transfers from the Arab states to institutions and individuals in the United States came from two main sources: the governments of the oil economies and American citizens employed in the Arab world. During the period under review, the governments of Saudi Arabia, the United Arab Emirates, Kuwait and Libya made direct and indirect grants to universities, research institutes and other institutions judged as playing a role in shaping public opinion and as participating in the political decision-making process in the United States. While the cumulative size of these transfers cannot be estimated, it may be assumed, on the basis of partial data published, that the amount in question is in the range of tens of millions of dollars.[11] The cumulative total of the transfers made by some 90,000 United States nationals (including military personnel) who in late 1977 served in administrative, advisory, instructional and supervisory positions in Saudi Arabia and other Arab states cannot be estimated.[12]

More than any other sphere, excepting actual American dependence on the OAPEC oil supply, economic relations between the United States and the Arab world were influenced by a flow of investments into the United States by a number of Arab oil

Table 2.7
US aid to Arab countries, 1974-78ᵃ (authorized grants, loans and technical assistance)

	1974		1975		1976ᵇ		1977		1978		Total 1974-78	
	$ mn	%	$ mn	%	$ mn	%	$ mn	%	$ mn	%	$ mn	%
Egypt												
Economic	21		371		1,032		898		919		3,241	
Military	–		–		–		–		–		–	
Total	21	11.5	371	37.1	1,032	65.0	898	66.8	919	67.7	3,241	59.2
Jordan												
Economic	65		99		144		75		99		482	
Military	42		105		133		145		132		557	
Total	107	58.8	204	20.4	277	17.4	220	16.4	231	17.0	1,039	19.0
Syria												
Economic	–		104		114		98		106		422	
Military	–		–		–		–		–		–	
Total	–	—	104		114	7.2	98	7.3	106	7.8	422	7.7
Lebanon												
Economic	5		–		10		46		54		115	
Military	10		–		–		–		25		35	
Total	15	8.2	–		10	0.6	46	3.4	79	5.8	150	2.7
Othersᶜ												
Economic	29		21		30		36		30		146	
Military	10		300		125		46		–		481	
Total	39	21.4	321	32.1	155	9.8	82	6.1	30	2.2	627	11.4
Total												
Economic	120		595		1,330		1,153		1,200		4,406	
Military	62		405		258		191		157		1,073	
Total	182	100.0	1,000	100.0	1,588	100.0	1,344	100.0	1,357	100.0	5,479	100.0

Notes: a US fiscal years.
b Includes interim quarter (1 July-30 September 1976).
c Partial data, includes mainly Morocco and Sudan.
Source: US, State Department, 1978.

Table 2.8

Net external assets of Arab oil exporting countries, 1976-78[a]
(estimates) (billions of dollars)

	1976	1977	1978
Saudi Arabia	56	68	77
Kuwait	25	31	38
United Arab Emirates	12	16	21
Libya	6	8	9
Iraq	5	7	8
Qatar	4	5	5
Total[b]	107	135	158

Notes:

a Figures for the end of the calendar year.

b Components may not add up to totals because of rounding.

Source:

Morgan Guaranty Trust Company, *World Financial Markets*, November 1977.

economies, led in this sphere too by Saudi Arabia. Six Arab oil producers (Saudi Arabia, Kuwait, the United Arab Emirates, Libya, Iraq and Qatar) managed, as a result of surpluses generated in their current accounts, to accumulate foreign assets whose real value was estimated in December 1976 at $107 billion and in December 1977 at $135 billion. The foreign assets of Saudi Arabia alone were estimated at the end of 1977 at $68 billion (see table 2.8).[13] According to various sources, total Arab public investment in the United States during 1974–77 amounted to at least $60–70 billion,[14] with the largest share owned by the Saudi Arabian government. Of this amount, $17.2 billion in 1976 and some $23 billion in 1977 were invested in United States bonds and long-term, nonnegotiable treasury notes.[15] In contrast to the considerable investments by the Arab oil states in the United States in 1977, American companies, according to an estimate by the United States Department of Commerce, invested only $2.9 billion in the Arab states that year, with the estimate of investment for previous years much lower.[16]

The aggregate inflow of dollars originating in the Arab states to the United States in 1974–77 was tens of billions of dollars greater than the outflow of dollars from the United States to the Arab economies. In other words, capital export from the Arab oil countries to the United States more than offset the deficit in the balance of trade and the possible deficit in the balance of invisible trade between the United States and the OAPEC economies, as well as the flow of net unilateral transfers and economic aid from the United States to the Arab world. This fact was of particular significance given the deficit in the overall current account of the United States and the weakness of the dollar in the world market during 1977.

Three additional facts are noteworthy in relation to American economic dependence on the Arab world. First, price-fixing of crude oil on the world market during the mid-1970s was the province of a group of Arab oil exporters who produced over 60 percent of the Opec oil then, with Saudi Arabia the main arbiter in fixing the price of Opec oil, given the size of its proven reserves and real production capacity. Second, the major United States allies in western Europe, and Japan, with whom it maintained the most extensive economic relations, themselves depended on OAPEC oil supplies to an even greater extent than did the United States itself (see table 2.9). Third, the intensification and diversification of American economic relations with the Arab states had an important microeconomic aspect. During the mid-1970s, some five hundred American companies (many of which were among the top one-hundred companies in the United States) in various branches of heavy and light industry, construction and engineering, minerals, banking and transportation maintained offices and staffs in the Arab states.[17] These companies in turn provided orders for hundreds of other American companies. American economic ties with the Arab states thus ensured employment for hundreds of thousands of workers in the industrial and service branches in the United States, and contributed to the increased business turnover and profitability of hundreds of companies.[18] All these factors created strong interests among broad and diverse groups in the American economy — from the shareholders and managements of the companies involved to the production line workers — in strengthening economic ties with the Arab economies, especially with Saudi Arabia.

ECONOMIC DEPENDENCE OF THE ARAB STATES ON THE UNITED STATES

The growing dependence of a number of Arab economies on income deriving from the export of oil gave rise to the argument

Table 2.9

Western Europe and Japan's imports of crude oil
and refined products from OAPEC, 1975-76

(estimates)

	1975			1976		
	Total imports	Imports from OAPEC		Total imports	Imports from OAPEC	
	'000 b/d	'000 b/d	%	'000 b/d	'000 b/d	%
	1	2	3(=1÷2)	4	5	6(=4÷5)
Britain	1,830	990	54.1	2,052	965	47.0
France	2,190	1,550	70.8	2,598	1,805	69.5
West Germany	1,970	1,170	59.4	2,809	1,276	45.4
Italy	1,990	1,420	71.4	2,268	1,196	52.7
Netherlands	1,200	580	48.3	1,435	691	48.2
Western Europe[a]	12,080	7,520	62.3	13,528	8,292	61.3
Japan	5,010	2,540	50.7	5,235	2,909	55.6

Note:

a In addition to the five countries listed, includes also Belgium, Luxembourg, Spain, Portugal, Austria, Switzerland, Denmark, Sweden and Norway.

Source:
US, Department of Energy, 1977.

among political analysts that these economies depended to a considerable extent on the rate of oil consumption in the United States, the second-largest consumer of OAPEC oil in absolute terms after Japan. This argument, however, requires qualifying, as it did not apply in periods of over-demand in the world oil market. Even in periods of over-supply, the argument was meaningful only in relation to two Arab oil exporters, Algeria and Libya. The relative share of the crude oil exports of each of these countries to the United States rose in 1976 to 41 percent of total oil exports for Algeria and 23 percent for Libya. Algerian dependence on American demand for its oil was particularly conspicuous in light of the deficit in both its balance of trade and its current account during the period under review.[19] The rate of crude oil exports by the rest of the OAPEC members to the United States did not exceed 13 percent (2.4 million barrels a day out of a total 18.8 million barrels; see table 2.10). The breakdown of export of crude oil and refined prooducts by OAPEC members shows an identical conclusion with regard to the extent of their dependence on the United States as a customer. Moreover, adding visible exports to the United States deriving from the non-oil sector of the Arab states does not alter the conclusion that the American market as consumer was of secondary importance for the Arab economies, with the exception of Algeria and Libya. The relative share of visible exports to the United States in 1976 from the oil economies of Kuwait and Iraq, as well as from Syria, Lebanon, Jordan and Morocco, totaled a mere 1 percent or less for each (see table 2.11).

The picture was somewhat different regarding the significance of the American economy as a source of visible imports for the Arab states. With the exception of Algeria, Libya, Bahrain, Oman and Tunisia, the relative share of visible imports from the United States in all the other Arab economies exceeded the relative share of visible exports to that country. The biggest importer from the United States in the Arab world in both absolute and relative terms was Saudi Arabia, which in 1976 imported goods at an overall value of about $3.1 billion, constituting some 26 percent of its total visible imports. Egypt was the second largest importer from the United States in the Arab world with, about $900 million, or approximately 18 percent of its total visible imports in 1976 (see table 2.11).

A high degree of interrelationship was apparent between the volume and rate of visible exports to the United States, as well as investment in that country, by Saudi Arabia and the United Arab Emirates, and the volume and rate of visible imports of these economies from the United States. The same interrelationship existed between Egypt and the United States. By contrast, there was a low degree of interrelationship between the high rates of visible exports by Algeria and Libya to the United States, and the low rates of visible imports by those two economies from the United States, while the opposite was true with regard to Kuwait, which had a low rate of visible exports to the United States but a high rate of visible imports from it.

About 74 percent of the visible imports by the Arab states from the United States consisted of finished industrial products and some 17 percent consisted of agricultural produce, leading to the claim that the dependence of the Arab states on American

45

Table 2.10

OAPEC crude oil exports — totals and to US, 1973-76
(annual averages)

		1973a		1974		1975		1976	
		'000 b/d	%	'000 b/d	%	'000 b/d	%	'000 b/d	%
Algeria	Total	1,070	100.0	960	100.0	960	100.0	990	100.0
	to U.S.	124	11.6	180	18.8	264	27.5	408	41.2
Egypt	Total	165	100.0	145	100.0	250	100.0	330	100.0
	to U.S.	—	—	9	6.2	5	2.0	17	5.2
Iraq	Total	2,020	100.0	1,970	100.0	2,260	100.0	2,415	100.0
	to U.S.	17	0.8	—	—	2	0.1	26	1.1
Kuwait	Total	3,020	100.0	2,545	100.0	2,085	100.0	2,145	100.0
	to U.S.	44	1.5	5	0.2	4	0.2	1	0.1
Libya	Total	2,175	100.0	1,520	100.0	1,480	100.0	1,935	100.0
	to U.S.	153	7.0	4	0.3	223	15.1	444	22.9
Qatar	Total	570	100.0	520	100.0	440	100.0	495	100.0
	to U.S.	41	7.2	17	3.3	18	4.1	24	4.8
Saudi Arabia	Total	7,595	100.0	8,480	100.0	7,075	100.0	8,575	100.0
	to U.S.	599	7.9	438	5.2	701	9.9	1,222	14.3
UAE	Total	1,535	100.0	1,680	100.0	1,665	100.0	1,935	100.0
	to U.S.	88	5.7	69	4.1	117	7.0	255	13.2
OAPEC	Total	18,150	100.0	17,820	100.0	16,215	100.0	18,820	100.0
	to U.S.	1,066	5.9	722	4.1	1,334	8.2	2,397	12.7

Notes:
a Figures for oil exports to US are averages for September 1973 (pre-crisis level).
Source:
US, Department of Energy, *Monthly Petroleum Statistics Reports*, 1977.

industry and agriculture was excessive. An analysis of the relevant data, however, leads to the conclusion that this argument too is in need of qualification. The rate of import of industrial products from the United States out of total industrial imports was high only in Saudi Arabia, which in 1976 imported 25 percent of its industrial products from the United States. In the other Arab economies this rate was lower (see table 2.6). Moreover, Saudi dependence on American industry was not great, for, apart from a limited number of products, mainly in the sphere of arms, substitutes for American imported items which were close in quality and either identical or cheaper in price were available from other industrialized economies. Furthermore, the relatively large share of industrial imports by Saudi Arabia from the United States did not derive from economic factors only. In view of intensive competition from 1975 onward between American companies and manufacturers in Japan, Britain, France, Germany, Italy and other countries for orders of industrial products by the Saudi government, with the manufacturers in those countries having obvious advantages over their American counterparts in many fields, the fact that American companies obtained more orders than manufacturers from other industrialized states was attributable in part to support offered them by the American government for trade activity with Saudi Arabia. An additional factor was the greater exposure of the Saudi rulers to American pressures than to pressures by other industrialized states.

Another claim was the great dependence of the Arab world on the import of wheat from the United States. The Arab economies together imported over half their total wheat consumption during the mid-1970s. However, even though the United States was the main purveyor of wheat to the Arab world, American wheat exports amounted to no more than 15–20 percent of total Arab wheat consumption. The breakdown of the import of wheat from the United States by country shows that only Algeria, Jordan and Saudi Arabia imported 30 percent or more of their total consumption from the United States.[20] Moreover, in high-yield years, other major wheat exporters — e.g., Canada, Australia and Argentina — could supply the total Arab demand for wheat without a sharp rise in price. No convincing parallel can be drawn, therefore, between American dependence on Arab oil and the Arab economies' dependence on industrial products or agricultural produce from the United States.

A pivotal aspect of this economic interrelationship, however,

Table 2.11
Arab countries' visible trade — totals and with US, 1972-76

		1972		1973		1974		1975		1976	
		$ mn	%	$ mn	%	$ mn	%	$ mn	%	$ mn	%
Algeria	Total	1,471.9	100.0	2,251.0	100.0	4,358.1	100.0	5,917.8	100.0	5,313.0	100.0
	US	103.0	7.0	185.0	8.2	346.2	7.9	695.0	11.7	632.1	11.9
Bahrain	Total	323.4	100.0	509.4	100.0	1,131.7	100.0	1,188.9	100.0	1,664.0	100.0
	US	29.2	9.0	43.9	8.6	80.3	7.1	91.8	7.7	145.1	8.7
Egypt	Total	888.8	100.0	908.3	100.0	2,351.7	100.0	3,534.0	100.0	4,983.7	100.0
	US	78.1	8.8	115.4	12.7	389.0	16.5	580.9	16.4	891.1	17.9
Iraq	Total	717.2	100.0	904.9	100.0	2,364.4	100.0	4,202.9	100.0	3,277.8	100.0
	US	29.1	4.1	50.3	5.6	188.2	8.0	370.3	8.8	163.2	5.0
Jordan	Total	270.9	100.0	327.7	100.0	432.2	100.0	732.6	100.0	925.3	100.0
	US	47.3	17.5	34.0	10.4	54.5	11.3	56.8	7.8	82.4	8.9
Kuwait	Total	797.0	100.0	1,043.0	100.0	1,556.0	100.0	2,388.0	100.0	3,648.0	100.0
	US	104.0	13.0	147.0	14.1	219.0	14.1	430.0	18.0	510.0	14.0
Lebanon	Total	859.6	100.0	1,252.5	100.0	2,438.9	100.0	2,141.4	100.0	820.4	100.0
	US	106.5	12.4	146.8	11.7	315.5	12.9	405.3	18.9	53.6	6.5
Libya	Total	1,044.5	100.0	1,722.9	100.0	2,762.8	100.0	4,035.3	100.0	4,774.9	100.0
	US	65.8	6.3	93.8	5.4	107.1	3.9	174.5	4.3	304.4	6.4

IMPORTS[a]

IMPORTS[a]

		1972 $ mn	1972 %	1973 $ mn	1973 %	1974 $ mn	1974 %	1975 $ mn	1975 %	1976 $ mn	1976 %
Morocco	Total	779.0	100.0	1,144.3	100.0	1,910.0	100.0	2,567.4	100.0	2,837.4	100.0
	US	58.9	7.6	120.6	10.5	170.2	8.9	196.9	7.7	241.5	8.5
Oman	Total	185.9	100.0	162.6	100.0	458.0	100.0	669.4	100.0	667.3	100.0
	US	7.3	3.9	10.2	6.3	40.5	8.8	64.6	9.6	44.0	6.6
Qatar	Total	138.4	100.0	194.4	100.0	270.9	100.0	577.4	100.0	973.4	100.0
	US	14.4	10.4	19.9	10.2	27.7	10.2	55.3	9.6	84.6	8.7
Saudi Arabia	Total	1,136.0	100.0	1,961.0	100.0	2,858.0	100.0	7,060.0	100.0	11,812.0	100.0
	US	221.0	19.5	380.0	19.4	489.0	17.1	1,652.0	23.4	3,051.0	25.8
Sudan	Total	338.6	100.0	436.1	100.0	710.7	100.0	1,033.4	100.0	980.5	100.0
	US	13.8	4.1	33.2	7.6	63.6	8.9	88.2	8.5	92.1	9.4
Syria	Total	539.6	100.0	613.2	100.0	1,229.7	100.0	1,685.5	100.0	2,428.1	100.0
	US	24.2	4.5	22.6	3.7	35.9	2.9	109.3	6.5	129.8	5.3
Tunisia	Total	459.6	100.0	606.3	100.0	1,135.6	100.0	1,421.8	100.0	1,493.9	100.0
	US	55.1	12.0	56.4	9.3	92.5	8.1	96.0	6.8	92.5	6.2
UAE	Total	495.6	100.0	838.7	100.0	1,781.8	100.0	2,754.5	100.0	3,419.7	100.0
	US	69.4	14.0	133.0	15.9	232.3	13.0	415.2	15.1	459.0	13.4
Yemen, AR	Total	80.8	100.0	122.3	100.0	189.8	100.0	293.9	100.0	412.4	100.0
	US	1.1	1.4	1.3	1.1	4.4	2.3	5.2	1.8	15.5	3.8
Yemen, PDR	Total	105.5	100.0	107.4	100.0	268.3	100.0	171.3	100.0	253.9	100.0
	US	1.0	0.9	3.3	3.1	13.6	5.1	3.1	1.8	5.5	2.2
Arab Countries	Total	10,632.3	100.0	15,106.0	100.0	28,258.6	100.0	42,375.5	100.0	50,685.5	100.0
	US	1,029.2	9.7	1,596.7	10.6	2,869.5	10.2	5,490.4	13.0	6,997.4	13.8

cont'd

		EXPORTS[b]									
		1972		1973		1974		1975		1976	
		$ mn	%	$ mn	%	$ mn	%	$ mn	%	$ mn	%
Algeria	Total	1,287.4	100.0	1,895.6	100.0	4,313.3	100.0	4,201.3	100.0	4,972.3	100.0
	US	108.8	8.5	210.0	11.1	1,091.1	25.3	1,359.6	32.4	2,111.2	42.5
Bahrain	Total	201.3	100.0	309.4	100.0	1,170.4	100.0	1,107.3	100.0	1,248.2	100.0
	US	20.0	9.9	18.1	5.8	129.3	11.0	251.7	22.7	119.0	9.5
Egypt	Total	825.2	100.0	1,124.7	100.0	1,516.3	100.0	1,576.3	100.0	2,285.7	100.0
	US	11.9	1.4	17.2	1.5	11.5	0.8	15.2	1.0	100.5	4.4
Iraq	Total	1,211.4	100.0	1,829.4	100.0	5,839.0	100.0	7,293.9	100.0	8,296.3	100.0
	US	16.3	1.3	16.7	0.9	2.0	—	20.7	0.3	111.8	1.3
Jordan	Total	47.6	100.0	57.4	100.0	153.4	100.0	152.6	100.0	207.1	100.0
	US		—		—		—		—		—
Kuwait	Total	2,906.0	100.0	3,790.0	100.0	10,961.0	100.0	9,186.0	100.0	8,256.0	100.0
	US	49.0	1.7	59.0	1.6	55.0	0.5	79.0	0.9	28.0	0.3
Lebanon	Total	354.4	100.0	608.4	100.0	1,455.4	100.0	1,206.8	100.0	795.5	100.0
	US	23.4	6.6	27.6	4.5	29.6	2.0	32.8	2.7	4.9	0.6
Libya	Total	2,308.2	100.0	3,996.3	100.0	8,260.8	100.0	5,866.1	100.0	8,232.3	100.0
	US	178.1	7.7	309.4	7.7	7.1	0.1	1,190.3	20.3	2,187.5	26.6
Morocco	Total	640.2	100.0	912.8	100.0	1,703.2	100.0	1,542.7	100.0	1,260.5	100.0
	US	10.4	1.6	12.7	1.4	18.1	1.1	11.4	0.7	14.2	1.1
Oman	Total	231.1	100.0	325.9	100.0	1,133.3	100.0	1,445.0	100.0	1,571.7	100.0
	US	6.7	2.9	6.1	1.9	33.1	2.9	127.2	8.8	248.0	15.8
Qatar	Total	394.2	100.0	622.5	100.0	1,524.1	100.0	1,422.6	100.0	1,989.4	100.0
	US	2.8	0.7	23.7	3.8	80.6	5.3	57.0	4.0	120.3	6.0

EXPORTS^b

		1972		1973		1974		1975		1976	
		$ mn	%	$ mn	%	$ mn	%	$ mn	%	$ mn	%
Saudi Arabia	Total	4,519.0	100.0	7,696.0	100.0	30,992.0	100.0	28,959.0	100.0	36,361.0	100.0
	US	224.0	5.0	376.0	4.9	1,085.0	3.5	2,623.0	9.1	5,315.0	14.6
Sudan	Total	357.9	100.0	436.7	100.0	350.4	100.0	439.4	100.0	554.2	100.0
	US	10.6	3.0	8.4	1.9	19.8	5.7	9.6	2.2	21.7	3.9
Syria	Total	287.3	100.0	351.0	100.0	784.3	100.0	930.0	100.0	1,045.2	100.0
	US	1.9	0.7	2.6	0.7	2.5	0.3	6.0	0.6	10.3	1.0
Tunisia	Total	310.9	100.0	384.4	100.0	925.9	100.0	857.5	100.0	787.3	100.0
	US	11.4	3.7	56.8	14.8	47.7	5.2	88.1	10.3	85.6	10.9
UAE	Total	803.5	100.0	1,575.0	100.0	5,274.0	100.0	5,947.0	100.0	8,507.3	100.0
	US	26.9	3.3	66.4	4.2	366.7	7.0	681.6	11.5	1,006.9	11.8
Yemen, AR	Total	4.4	100.0	7.8	100.0	13.3	100.0	10.9	100.0	7.7	100.0
	US	—		—		—		0.2	1.8	—	
Yemen, PDR	Total	39.8	100.0	84.7	100.0	230.0	100.0	282.3	100.0	288.5	100.0
	US	2.7	6.8	4.0	4.7	6.8	3.0	1.4	0.5	0.9	0.3
Arab Countries	Total	16,729.8	100.0	26,008.0	100.0	76,600.1	100.0	72,426.7	100.0	86,666.2	100.0
	US	704.9	4.2	1,214.7	4.7	2,986.0	3.8	6,554.9	9.0	11,485.9	13.3

Notes:
a C.i.f. or f.o.b., according to the countries' reports to the IMF.
b F.o.b.

Source:
IMF, *Direction of Trade, Annual 1970-76*, 1977.

was the degree of dependence of the Arab states on the United States in all matters connected with the acquisition of up-to-date know-how and technology and the training of skilled manpower. The approximately 90,000 American citizens employed in the Arab states during 1977 (about 70,000 of whom were in Saudi Arabia) were engaged in the planning, administration and supervision of a wide range of projects, from transportation infrastructure to the establishment and operation of research institutes and universities. Furthermore, there was a clear, large-scale flow of Arab students to the United States for the acquisition of higher education. An estimate of the total number of students from the Arab states who studied for academic degrees in the United States in 1977 was about 30,000 (of whom about 8,000 were from Saudi Arabia).[21] Even if the various universities in the Western world apart from the United States could absorb that number of Arab students, they could not offer the range of curricula available in the United States which were sought after by the Arab governments supporting students abroad. In addition, there was an obvious connection between the scope of activity of American companies in the Arab states and the number of nationals of those countries who acquired technical and higher education in the United States.

An aditional factor contributing to economic interdependence was the assets held by the Arab oil states in the United States, which gave them a vested interest in monetary stability and a high growth rate in the American economy. A high rate of inflation in the United States, by contrast, would mean a decline in the real value of securities, bonds and treasury notes. Saudi Arabia's interest in the maintenance of monetary stability and high growth rates in the United States explains, at least partially, its 1976–77 policy regarding the fixing of crude oil prices on the world market as well as its own production of oil. During the Opec oil ministers conferences of 1976–77, Saudia Arabia adamantly opposed sharp rises in the price of crude oil, a stand which conflicted with that of most of the other Opec members.

The varied extent of the Arab countries' economic dependence on the United States during 1973–77 may be categorized in three groups: (1) economies with a high rate of dependence, including Algeria (the American oil market); Egypt and Jordan (economic aid); and Saudi Arabia and the United Arab Emirates (industrial imports, technology and investments in the United States); (2) economies with a low rate of dependence, including Iraq, Sudan and South Yemen; and (3) other economies with a degree of dependence that was not of great significance, including Libya, Qatar, Oman, Bahrain, Syria, Lebanon, Tunisia, Morocco and North Yemen.

AN ASYMMETRICAL ECONOMIC INTERDEPENDENCE

Data on the economic relationship between the United States and the Arab countries point to a growing expansion in the mid-1970s, with economic interdependence taking on unprecedented forms. Gradually, however, this interdependence became clearly asymmetrical in that American dependence on the Arab states was greater, and perhaps more critical, than vice versa, since it hinged on the import of a rew material vital to any industrialized economy.

The United States was particularly dependent on Saudi Arabia, which in the mid-1970s became the biggest oil supplier of the American economy. The dependence of the Arab economies on the United States in certain fields, by contrast, did not involve the rare combination of a vital raw material and an absence of suitable substitutes for it in the short term. This asymmetry was based on the fact that, all other things being equal, the American economy was not capable of functioning properly without the import of Arab oil, while the Arab economies, including Saudi Arabia's, if bereft of their economic relations with the United States, would have been only partially damaged.

Fortunately for the United States, the political conditions in the Middle East in general and in the Arabian Peninsula in particular presented possibilities for offsetting this economic asymmetry. The inherent weakness of the oil state regimes of the Arabian Peninsula, and their hostility toward and fear of the growing threat of both internal and external radical forces, prompted them to strengthen their political ties with the United States, to the extent that the stability of these regimes was dependent on the political and military support of the United States. The administration in Washington responded with unqualified enthusiasm to this orientation on the part of the oil states in the Arabian Peninsula, led by Saudi Arabia, undertaking to guarantee the security of Saudi Arabia and its neighbors in the peninsula against external threats. Thus, a situation developed from 1973 onward in which the asymmetry of American economic dependence on Arab oil in the Arabian Peninsula was offset by an asymmetry in the political dependence of these oil states on the United States.

NOTES

1. The Arab economies discussed in this chapter are (in alphabetical order): Algeria, Bahrain, Egypt, Iraq, Jordan, Kuwait, Lebanon, Libya, Morocco, Oman, Qatar, Saudi Arabia, Sudan, Syria, Tunisia, the United Arab Emirates, North Yemen (San'a) and South Yemen (Aden).
2. United States Department of Commerce, FT 135.
3. On US aid to Egypt, see table 2.7, below.
4. "Japan Scores with Cheaper Goods Delivered Faster," *MEED*, Special Report: Japan, October 1977, p. ix; Gardiner Brown, "Rising Costs of Oil Imports Challenge US Export Lead," *MEED*, Special Report: Arab-American Commerce, November 1977, p. 14.
5. For an estimate of the real value of the Arab oil countries' assets in the United States, see table 2.8, below.
6. My estimate is based on data published by SAMA, *Statistical Summary, 1975/6*; *International Financial Statistics* 29/12 (1976); *U.S. Federal Reserve Bulletin*, February 1977; Morgan Guarantee Trust Company, *World Financial Markets*, November 1977.
7. See the list of American oil companies operating in Arab countries, *MEED*, Special Report, November 1977, pp. 31-33.
8. See the list of leading American construction companies operating in Arab countries, ibid., p. 22.
9. Ibid., pp. 18-27.
10. My estimate is based on data published in *Oil and Gas International Yearbook 1977*; *Engineering News Record*, 15 April 1976, 14 April 1977; *PE* 44 (1977): 92-93, 177-78, 242, 362, 363. See also *MEED*, Special Report, November 1977, p. 14.
11. See, e.g., *Petroeconomic File*, no. 14, March 1978.
12. United States Senate Committee on Energy and Natural Resources, *Access to Oil — The United States Relationships with Saudi Arabia and Iran*, no. 95-70, December 1977, p. 40; *MEED*, Special Report, November 1977, p. 68; *New York Times*, 8 January 1978.
13. Cf. *MEED*, 20 January 1978, p. 4.
14. *al-Sayyad*, 19 February 1976; *Middle East Currency Reports* 3/7 (May 1977): 29-32.
15. *Middle East Currency Reports* 3/7 (May 1977): 29-32; *MEED*, 20 January 1978, p. 4.
16. *MEED*, Special Report, November 1977, p. 13.
17. Ibid., p. 11.
18. Ibid., p. 13.
19. IMF, *Direction of Trade, Annual 1970-1976*, August 1977, p. 63; id., *Balance of Payments Yearbook*, 1975-77.
20. FAO, *World Wheat Statistics*, 1976; US, *Foreign Agricultural Trade Statistics*, 1976.
21. *MEED*, Special Report, November 1977, p. 177; *Time*, 29 May 1978, p. 19; *Tishrin*, 25 and 27 February 1978.

3

The "New-Old" Economic Order
in the Middle East

FOUR REGIONAL BLOCS

Rapid population growth and a massive inflow of capital from abroad — the two dominant socioeconomic developments in the Middle East in the 1970s and 1980s — determined a division of the region into four demographic-economic blocs of states. This division holds the key to understanding the major political developments of the last two decades, including the Gulf War in 1991. A basic aspect of this demographic-economic division is that while the first process — rapid demographic growth — was common to almost all Middle Eastern societies, the second — massive inflow of capital from abroad — occurred in only half the states in the region, directly affecting only about a third of the overall population of the region.

The four blocs of states may be defined both by demographic-economic and by geographic attributes:

(1) The "western Middle East bloc": Egypt, Sudan and Yemen. During the 1970s and 1980s these states were characterized by high natural increase rates on the one hand, and low economic growth rates on the other. Since these processes occurred in societies where the GNP per capita during the first half of the century was already very low, the economies in question became so impoverished that this bloc contained the poorest societies in the Middle East in terms of GNP per capita. In South Yemen in 1988 this figure stood at $430, in Sudan $480, in North Yemen $640 and in Egypt $660.[1] These four economics were counted among the 50 poorest states in the world (those with GNP per capita of less than $800)[2] that year. The processes outlined

55

above aggravated population pressure on available economic resources during the 1980s. Housing and unemployment problems meant severe hardship for millions of people in these countries.

(2) The "central Middle East bloc": the oil states of the Arabian Peninsula. The largest and most important of these was Saudi Arabia, and the others were Kuwait, the United Arab Emirates and the three oil principalities — Qatar, Oman and Bahrain. Most of these states were characterized by high rates of natural increase. Their populations also increased because of a migratory movement to them, although this was temporary in part as some migrants returned to their country of origin and others failed to obtain local citizenship. In any event, these were societies with relatively small populations in absolute terms at the end of the 1980s. Saudi Arabia had a domestic population of no more than 8–10 million at the end of the 1980s,[3] while the other polities in this bloc numbered two million persons or less each.[4] Parallel with the growth in their populations, these economies enjoyed high economic growth rates in the 1970s and early 1980s. These were markedly higher than the rates of population growth, resulting in a steep rise in GNP per capita. This figure amounted to $6,200 in Saudi Arabia in 1988, $13,400 in Kuwait, and $15,770 in the United Arab Emirates, placing these three economies among the 25 richest states ("high-income economies") in the world in the late 1980s.[5]

(3) The "eastern Middle East bloc": Iran and Iraq. These two states differed notably in certain demographic-economic features, but had several important attributes in common that set them apart from the other states of the region. Both had comparatively large populations. Iran's was over 50 million at the end of the 1980s and Iraq's about 17 million,[6] making it the most highly populated Arab state in the Asian continent. The populations in both countries grew at high rates in the last generation, with the rise in rates of natural increase particularly marked during the 1980s in both. Demographically, there was a similarity between this bloc and the western bloc, while in terms of capital inflow there was a similarity to the central bloc. Iran and Iraq were also large oil exporters, among the largest producing and exporting states in the Middle East and in Opec. However, owing to population size and political developments in the 1980s, income from oil exports did not result in the same rise in GNP per capita as in the central bloc. GNP per capita in these two states was higher than in the western bloc, but considerably lower than in the central bloc: about $3,000 in Iraq in 1988 and about $2,000 in Iran.[7]

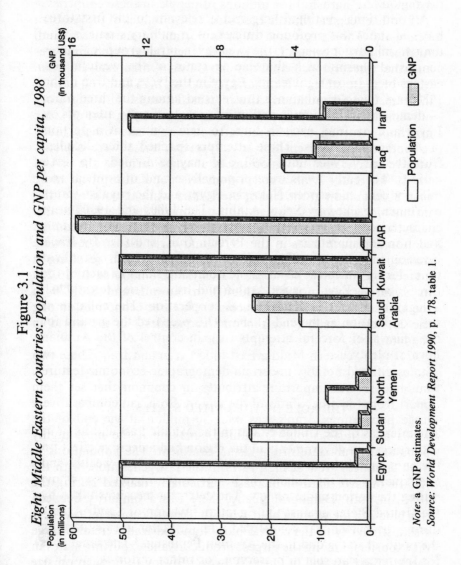

Figure 3.1

Eight Middle Eastern countries: population and GNP per capita, 1988

Note: a GNP estimates.

Source: World Development Report 1990, p. 178, table 1.

(4)   The "northern bloc": the Levant states and Turkey. These were non-oil states, but were not among the poorest countries of the region.

An additional distinguishing factor relevant to the first three blocs of states was profound differences in military strength. The limited military power of the wealthy central group of states contrasted sharply with the leading states of the western and eastern blocs (most significantly Egypt in the 1960s and Iraq in the 1980s). A twofold imbalance thus existed among the three blocs — demographic-economic, and military — leading to attempts by Egypt and by Iraq, each in turn, to gain control of a portion of the Arabian riches. These attempts spanned three decades, from the early 1960s until 1990, and may be divided into three periods. The early 1960s were principally a time of political and military conflict between Nasserist Egypt and the royalist forces of Yemen, backed by Saudi Arabia. The 1980s and 1990s were characterized first by the prolonged bloody conflict between Iraq and Iran for supremacy in the Persian Gulf, and then by Iraq's invasion into Kuwait. The 1970s constituted a kind of twilight time, during which the elites in the dominant states in each of the three blocs — Egypt, Saudi Arabia and Iran — tried to establish a regional order based on mutual cooperation. The collapse of this cooperation at the end of the 1970s prepared the ground for the renewal of forceful attempts to gain control of the Arabian horn of plenty.

THE ROLE OF THE UNITED STATES

The interests of the United States in the Middle East and its links with rulers and governments in the region had a decisive effect on the outcome of the struggle over the sources of Arab wealth, and consequently on the balance of power in the region as a whole during the period under review. The deterrent measures taken by the United States against the Egyptian invasion of Saudi Arabia during the Yemen war constituted a major factor in safeguarding the political status quo in the Arabian Peninsula.[8] The same goes for the American role in preserving, or rather restoring, political order in the Arabian Peninsula in light of Iraqi ambitions and moves in the summer of 1990.

Signals emanating from Washington had a similar effect on moves made in the 1970s and 1980s by the dominant states of the three blocs. It is doubtful, for example, that Saudi Arabia would have so sharply reduced the scope of its assistance to Egypt in the second half of the 1970s had this not been acceptable to the United States administration. A different kind of example was the ambivalent signals sent to Baghdad from Washington immediately preceding the invasion of Kuwait, leading Saddam Husayn to believe that America would not respond in the event of an Iraqi onslaught.

The multi-faceted and consistent American involvement in protecting the political status quo in the Arabian Peninsula had several motives, the most important of which was American dependence on the oil produced in the Middle East generally and by the "Saudi group" in particular. The import of crude oil from the Middle East by the American economy assumed large dimensions in the 1970s and 1980s, albeit with strong fluctuations.[9] The Saudi group exerted a determining influence on the oil price level in the world market during this period by virtue of the huge proven oil reserves located in their territory, totaling about 50 percent of the world's proven oil reserves in 1989.[10] For a long time the Saudi oil industry and that of its neighbors in the Peninsula possessed a high unexploited production capacity, which in effect enabled the maintenance of a low price level even in times of crisis. From the American viewpoint, a constant, assured and regular flow of crude oil from the Saudi group to the Western economies was of supreme importance, while disruptions in this supply were a nightmare to any administration in Washington because of the serious consequences to an economic system highly dependent on energy derived from oil.

The existing demographic-economic imbalance in the oil states of the Arabian Peninsula in particular and in the Middle East in general held great advantages for the United States. The obvious disproportion in Saudi Arabia, Kuwait and the United Arab Emirates between great economic wealth on the one hand and limited military power on the other, exacerbated by serious threats from neighbors claiming an ideological right to the oil wells, impelled the rulers of these states to huddle together under the American defense umbrella. As external threats mounted, the dependence of the Arabian Peninsula regimes on the readiness of the United States to defend them grew, a situation epitomized by the Iraqi capture of Kuwait. Through the advantage it had gained from this dependency the United States was able to safeguard its foremost interest in the region: oil. To perpetuate this advantage, it was imperative to prevent control over the oil of the Arabian Peninsula from falling into the hands of any state or elite that could muster sufficient military power or cherished aspirations for regional leadership. For thirty years the House of Sa'ud and the Sabah family were the favored partners as world suppliers of crude oil, rather than rulers of Nasser's or Saddam Husayn's sort.

It is noteworthy that Israel played no part in the struggles over control of the Peninsula oil. It had no direct influence on the course of developments in the two confrontations noted — the Yemen War and the Kuwait War — and even less on their outcomes. Its nonintervention was most remarkable in the Gulf War, considering the desperate Iraqi attempt to draw Israel into the conflict. Conversely, Israel's relations with several Arab states were affected positively by the results of the struggles under review. This applies especially to two developments: first, the change in Egypt's position toward Israel following the decline of the Cairo-Riyadh axis in 1976,[11] and second, the evolving change in the position of the Saudi bloc states toward Israel following the Iraqi invasion of Kuwait.[12]

CONCLUSION

The economic factor that drove neighboring states in the "western" and "eastern" regional blocs to seek control over various tracts of the Arabian Peninsula ultimately proved to be the force that blocked these attempts. Oil was the motive for direct and indirect efforts at seizure by Egypt and Iraq, but it was oil too that moved the United States to frustrate these efforts and to sustain and ensure the political status quo in the Arabian Peninsula. The sovereignty and territorial integrity of the Saudi bloc states were secured despite, but also by virtue of, the oil they possessed. In other words, oil was one of the factors that served to retain the political status quo in the Arab world and in the Middle East as a whole from the early 1960s onwards.

During this period, and especially from 1973, a chain of counterbalancing forces enveloped the "world's oil well," and despite occasional strife ensured the maintenance of the status quo. This chain consisted of three regional blocs and a distant superpower connected by its economy to that well. It should be pointed out that the efforts of this superpower to create a balance of forces in the three-bloc system to insure the status quo in the Arabian Peninsula did not always succeed. The most serious error in the 1980s was very likely its failure to foster the Cairo-Riyadh axis. Clearly, the "western" and "central" blocs greatly complemented each other with regard to demographic-economic balance. Moreover, the leading states in these two blocs were status-quo states during the 1970s and 1980s, a common denominator of major importance in any consideration of the political order in the Middle East. Indeed, regarding the United States, Saudi Arabia and Egypt, all their policies and activities in the context of the "new" economic order in the Middle East are essentially aimed at the consolidation and reinforcement of the "old" order, namely the strengthening of the status-quo forces to protect the existing regimes in the Arabian Peninsula.

NOTES

1. *World Development Report 1990*, p. 178, table 1.
2. Ibid.
3. For estimates on the size of the local population in Saudi Arabia see and compare Ramon Knauerhase, *The Saudi Arabian Economy*, New York: Praeger, 1975, pp. 12-13; J.S. Birks and C.A. Sinclair, *The International Migration Project, Country Case Study, The Kingdom of Saudi Arabia*, Durham: University of Durham, 1978, p. 15; UN, ESCWA, *Demographic and Related Socio-Economic Data Sheets*, Amman: UN-ESCWA, 1993, p. 120, table 1.
4. UN, *Demographic Yearbook 1990*, New York: UN, 1992, pp. 165-68, table 5 (hereafter: *Demographic Yearbook*).
5. *World Development Report 1990*, Ibid.
6. *Demographic Yearbook 1990*, ibid.
7. *World Development Report 1990*, ibid.
8. Nadav Safran, *Saudi Arabia. The Ceaseless Quest for Security*, Ithaca and London: Cornell University Press, 1988, pp. 110-11, 121-22.
9. See above, pp. 32-36; see also US Energy Information Administration, *Monthly Energy Review*, August 1990, tables 3.1 and 3.3.
10. *BP Statistical Review of Energy*, July 1990.
11. See below pp. 67-69.
12. See, for example, *'Ukaz*, 9 April 1991.

4

The Oil Boom and Pan-Arabism

From the early 1920s, when the institutional foundations of separate Arab nation-states in the Middle East were being laid, until the late 1970s, the Arab world existed in a state of tension between the conflicting pulls of Pan-Arabism and particularism. Several factors determined the course of events that unfolded between these two poles — between the creation of a single, unified Arab state on the one hand, and the consolidation of a number of such states on the other. Two specific developments — one of them demographic and the other economic — had a particular effect upon the tension between Arab unity and particularism: the high rate of natural increase of the Egyptian population, and the influence of the substantial revenues generated by the export of crude oil during the 1973–82 period. The interrelation between these developments had an impact inter alia on the situation of the separate Arab nation-state.

POPULATION GROWTH

The growth rates of the Arab population in the Middle East remained high during the last four decades. Indeed, in some Arab countries not only was there no drop in the rate of natural increase, but this rate actually rose significantly. Whatever our reservations concerning the reliability of the demographic data furnished by some of the governments in the region, natural increase rates of 3.0 percent and higher appear to have existed throughout the 1960s and 1970s in Syria, Iraq, Jordan, Libya

62

and apparently in the oil states of the Arabian Peninsula as well (see table 4.1).

A significant case in point is the recorded rise in the rate of natural increase in Egypt, from 2.2-2.3 percent early in the 1970s to about 2.7 percent in the late 1970s and early 1980s.[1] These high population growth rates were reflected in substantial absolute figures: between 1952 and 1985 Egypt's population increased from about 21 million to about 48 million.[2]

Rapid population growth has became a serious economic and social problem in Egypt, creating mounting pressures on available resources.[3] For a number of years when GDP growth rates were low (1966–68 and 1972), per capita growth rates in real terms were negative as a result of the high rates of population growth.[4] Rapid population growth was one of the factors accounting for the failure of repeated efforts to achieve self-sustained economic growth. The Egyptian government had in fact been aware since the mid-1950s, and possibly earlier, that the natural increase rate of the country's population demanded vigorous steps toward changing the structure of the economy and stimulating economic

Table 4.1

Eleven Arab countries: crude birthrates, crude death rates
and crude natural increase rates, 1960, 1970 and 1980
(per thousand)

	1960			1970			1980		
	CBR	CDR	CNIR	CBR	CDR	CNIR	CBR	CDR	CNIR
Sudan	46.5	24.5	22.0	46.7	22.1	24.6	46.8	18.7	28.1
Yemen, AR	49.7	28.9	20.8	48.8	26.5	22.3	48.5	23.2	25.3
Yemen, PDR	50.4	28.8	21.6	48.6	24.2	24.4	47.9	20.0	27.9
Egypt	43.5	19.0	24.5	38.5	15.1	23.4	36.6	12.1	24.5
Syria	47.0	17.7	29.3	46.5	13.5	33.0	47.1	8.1	39.0
Jordan	47.4	19.9	27.5	47.6	15.5	32.1	46.6	9.4	37.2
Iraq	49.4	19.9	29.5	48.1	15.8	32.3	47.0	12.4	34.6
Libya	49.0	19.3	29.7	50.7	15.6	35.1	47.1	12.1	35.0
Saudi Arabia	48.9	22.5	26.4	47.9	18.1	29.8	45.6	13.8	31.8
Kuwait	44.4	9.7	34.7	48.2	5.7	42.5	39.3	4.2	35.1
UAE	45.6	19.0	26.6	35.8	11.1	24.7	29.9	7.3	22.6

Source:
WB, *World Tables* 1983.

growth.[5] Moreover, Nasser realized that unless Egypt received large-scale aid from abroad, no real long-term economic growth could be achieved. He skillfully acquired economic aid during the 1960s and 1970s from virtually all the countries which had the economic capacity and political interest to offer it, namely the Soviet Union and the East European states; the United States and certain West European countries; and the Arab oil-producing states, chiefly Saudi Arabia.

ARAB OIL REVENUES

Oil revenues received by the Arab oil-producing countries were considerable even before the 1973 energy crisis. In 1969 the oil incomes of the two leaders in the field, Saudi Arabia and Libya, came to more than a billion dollars each. However, these revenues cannot be compared with those attained in the boom years of 1973–82, when total income accruing to OAPEC members (Saudi Arabia, Iraq, Kuwait, Libya, the United Arab Emirates, Algeria and Qatar) from the export of crude oil was $865 billion (see table 4.2). Of these countries, Saudi Arabia had the highest income: $428 billion.

These incomes were in excess of both the immediate needs of these economies and the opportunities available to them for short-

Table 4.2
OAPEC oil revenues, 1973-82
(billions of dollars)

	1973	1974	1975	1976	1977	1978	1979	1980	1981	1982
Saudi Arabia	4.3	22.6	25.7	33.5	38.6	34.6	57.5	102.0	113.2	76.0
Iraq	1.8	5.7	7.5	8.5	9.8	9.6	21.3	26.0	10.4	9.5
Kuwait	1.9	7.0	7.5	8.5	7.9	8.0	16.7	17.9	14.9	10.0
Libya	2.3	6.0	5.1	7.5	8.9	8.6	15.2	22.6	15.6	14.0
UAR	0.9	5.5	6.0	7.0	9.0	8.0	12.9	19.5	18.7	16.0
Algeria	0.9	3.7	3.4	3.7	4.3	4.6	7.5	12.5	10.8	8.5
Qatar	0.4	1.6	1.7	2.0	2.0	2.0	3.6	5.4	5.3	4.2
Total	12.5	52.1	56.9	70.7	80.5	75.4	134.7	205.9	188.9	138.2

Source:
PE, May 1977, p. 167; June 1981, p. 232; July 1985, p. 236.

term spending on consumption and investment, with the result that these countries began to accumulate enormous monetary reserves. At the end of 1981, these reserves of the Arab oil economies totalled $321 billion, with Saudi Arabia's reserves alone estimated at $160 billion.[6]

By the late 1970s, a deepening economic gap had opened between the populations on either side of the Red Sea — that of the Nile Valley and that of the Arabian Peninsula (except for the southeastern corner). Its impact was considerable, and meant among other things a weakening of the forces calling for Arab unity while it favored the "territorial" Arab nation-states.

Because of Egypt's need to turn to Arab oil producers for aid, initially for the purpose of arms procurement and later in order to finance economic projects, the country's leadership was forced, by the late 1960s, to desist from activities that might have undermined the stability of regimes which did not actively espouse the cause of Arab unity and especially not a union under Egyptian leadership. This decline in the type of Egyptian Nasserist activism characteristic of the late 1950s and early 1960s made it possible for regimes such as Saudi Arabia and Jordan, which sought to foster the development of the distinct nation-state, to pursue their ends. In addition, the failure of Nasserism, particularly its vision of Pan-Arabism, weakened Egypt's ideological opposition to the existence of separate Arab states.[7]

Meanwhile, those groups and sectors within the oil states that had a vested interest in the prevalence of a distinct nation-state saw their fortunes enhanced by the expanding revenues accruing to the oil states. Two groups that benefited specifically from increasing numbers and a growing share of political influence were the bureaucracy-technocracy, and the officer corps. Broadly, the public sector as a whole gained in a similar fashion.

The enormous investments of the Arab oil economies in economic development from 1974 — in infrastructure, industry, agriculture and human resources — were implemented mainly by means of the public sector. This required a considerable expansion of the number of workers employed in public service. According to one estimate, the number of persons employed in the civil service in Saudi Arabia (Saudi nationals receiving a monthly salary) grew from 20,000 in 1960 to about 184,000 in 1980. The number of Saudi teachers in the country's school system increased in the same period from 2,413 to 37,954.[8] Deriving their economic and social power from the Saudi political entity and from the various economic, social and political institutions that the state had established in recent decades, these groups naturally identified themselves with the Saudi state.[9]

Alongside the public sector, a broad group of private businessmen emerged in Saudi Arabia, as in the other oil economies, particularly merchants and suppliers of various services, becoming integral in the economic system that had been developing since 1974. The number of people employed in trade and finance in particular rose significantly from the early 1970s onward. The total figure for persons employed in services in the private sector increased from 253,000 in 1967 to 685,000 in 1979.[10]

The incomes of these socioeconomic groups, especially of those in the upper levels, rose in both absolute and relative terms after the Saudi government initiated its first five-year plan for economic development (1970–75).[11] Thus, these groups too developed a strong interest in the existence of a separate Saudi state. Clearly, the Saudi elite, like its counterparts in other oil-producing states in the Arabian Peninsula, was reluctant to share the economic resources at its disposal with the elites of other societies or states, even if they were Arab. Obviously, the greater the extent of such resources, the more reluctant the elite was to surrender control of it.

EGYPT AND ARAB AID

When Egypt set out to achieve economic growth during the 1970s and 1980s and sought rapprochement with the oil states of the Arab Peninsula, relations soon took on a different hue. At stake during 1974–77 was the issue of the scale and conditions of economic aid for Egypt. It is worth noting that the oil-producing Arab states, principally Saudi Arabia and Kuwait, had been extending aid to Egypt from 1967, as a consequence of the Khartoum summit.[12] But aid in significant amounts — of over a billion dollars annually — was granted to Egypt only after the 1973 war and the attendant precipitation of the energy crisis.

The sudden increase in income from oil exports at the end of 1973 and the beginning of 1974 elicited expectations among the Arab countries which were not major oil-exporters, particularly Egypt, of receiving generous amounts of economic aid from Saudi Arabia and Kuwait. These expectations were encouraged by a pan-Arab ideology which held, at least implicitly, that whatever natural resources existed in Arab territory had to be placed at the disposal of the whole Arab community.[13]

66

Other factors also nourished the Egyptian leadership's expectations of comprehensive economic aid. First, Egyptian spokesmen argued that the steep rise in the price of oil on the international market in October 1973 was, to a large extent, due to a war that had been initiated and led by Egypt. Second, for years Egypt had been in the forefront of the Arab struggle with Israel and in the course of that conflict Egypt had paid dearly in human lives — more than any other Arab state. Moreover, the economic cost to Egypt of the long, drawn-out conflict had been substantial. Estimating the direct cost to Egypt, Egyptian leaders cited figures of $12-15 billion, for which, they claimed, Egyptian society deserved to be properly compensated. Third, inasmuch as the major countries in the Middle East that were geographically close to Egypt had invested heavily in developing their economies from 1973, with the result that they had undergone tangible and extensive social and economic transformations, it was incumbent upon Egypt to keep up with them in its own development, and on a scale that would require economic aid from them.[14]

In the event, Egypt did receive large amounts of Arab aid during the period between the war in 1973 and the Baghdad foreign ministers' meeting in 1979. According to informed estimates, this aid — part of which was allocated to defense expenditures and part to civil needs — came to a total of $11-12 billion for this period.[15] The aid estimates published by various sources emanating from the Arab oil-producing states in 1979, when these countries' relations with Egypt were deteriorating, are even higher, amounting to as much as $17 billion,[16] although this figure would seem to be excessively high. While the unavailability of precise data makes it difficult to provide accurate figures on the relative share of military and defense aid made available to Egypt, a rough estimate would be 40-50 percent of total Arab aid.[17] Economic aid for civil purposes reached a peak in 1975, when it totalled over $2.0 billion.[18] The principal donor of this aid was Saudi Arabia, which made available a total of about $7 billion to Egypt during 1973-78.[19] Other major donors were Kuwait and the United Arab Emirates.

The aid officially extended to Egypt by Arab governments during the oil decade ended in 1979 in reaction to Sadat's peace initiative. However, a crisis had been brewing for some time in Egypt's relations with the countries from which it had been receiving aid, in particular Saudi Arabia. As early as the end of 1974 and the beginning of 1975, Egyptian statesmen began to

67

complain about the meagerness of the aid that was being offered by the Arab oil producers. Egyptian disappointment deepened in the course of 1975-76 against a background of governmental hopes that the oil-producing states of the Arabian Peninsula would offer Egypt $10-12 billion in aid for development projects related to its five-year plan for 1975–80.[20] This plan was supposed to reinvigorate the Egyptian economy, which had been in a state of stagnation since the mid-1960s in terms of gross investment and per capita growth rates. The response of the rulers of Saudi Arabia and Kuwait, however, was to establish GODE (the Gulf Organization for the Development of Egypt) in April 1976, an organization committed to help Egypt to get loans (rather than unilateral transfers) amounting to no more than $2 billion, to be received during a period of five years.[21]

In January of 1977 Egypt was struck by a wave of protests and demonstrations, known as the "food riots," which seriously threatened the stability of the Sadat regime.[22] These events, however, did not bring about any real change in Saudi or the other Arab oil states' attitudes on the matter of economic aid to Egypt. Newspapers in Kuwait even claimed that the "food riots" had been instigated by the Egyptian government itself in order to bring pressure to bear on the Arab oil states to increase their aid to Egypt, and ought not be taken seriously.[23] By 1976 Arab grants to Egypt had been scaled down significantly and the conditions attached to it made more stringent.[24]

The policy adopted by the rulers of Saudi Arabia and the other oil-producing states of the Peninsula during 1976–77 caused considerable resentment and bitterness in Egyptian government circles. Arab economic aid was being steadily reduced, and a forecast prepared by the Egyptian Ministry of Finance before November 1977 predicted a continuing decline for 1978, anticipating a reduction to a mere $300 million per annum by 1979.[25] This development prompted Egyptian statesmen in 1977 to accuse Saudi Arabia and its partners in GODE of humiliating conduct unbecoming to relations between two Arab states.[26]

Material published in the late 1970s and early 1980s seems to indicate that in the months following the January 1977 food riots, and possibly even earlier, Sadat reached two conclusions concerning the economic future of Egypt and its relations with the oil-producing states of the Arabian Peninsula. The first was that unless the country could achieve a sufficiently high economic growth rate, not only would the "New Egypt" — Egypt after the

July 1952 revolution — fail to fulfill the people's expectations, but the very regime whose foundations the Free Officers had laid would be seriously jeopardized. Second, the economic aid which had been furnished by the Arab oil states, and which in 1973–74 had been regarded by the Egyptian government as crucially important to Egypt's economic and social recovery, would no longer play the major role that had been anticipated in the country's renewed economic growth. The Egyptian leadership apparently reached the conclusion that the Saudi and Kuwaiti elites had no interest in a fundamental change in the Egyptian economy,[27] and that new sources of aid on an appropriate scale had to be sought elsewhere.

Significantly, these developments took place at a time when considerable monetary reserves were being accumulated by the oil producers, principally by Saudi Arabia, whose total aid to Egypt (about $7 billion) accounted for 4.4 percent of its total oil revenues in 1973–78 ($159 billion). The total aid of the three main donors — Saudi Arabia, Kuwait and the United Arab Emirates — (about $11 billion) accounted for 4.7 percent of their total revenues in the same period ($237 billion). Taking the entire period of the oil decade into account, the aid given to Egypt by Saudi Arabia alone and by the group of three donors together amounted to 1.1 percent of their total oil revenues ($7 billion out of $626 billion, and $11 billion out of $986 billion, respectively).

Saudi and Kuwaiti policy on the issue of economic aid appears to have reinforced the awareness of the Egyptian leadership, as well as of other social groups in the country, regarding the limits of implementing the idea of Pan-Arabism. Once this conclusion had been reached, no serious impediments remained — including those of an ideological nature — remained to ignoring a fundamental imperative of Arab nationalism: neither to recognize nor come to terms with the existence of Israel. The dramatic increase in incomes from the export of crude oil, and the expectations that this development elicited on both sides of the Red Sea, thus served to bring out an abiding fact of general political life: every country looks out for its own interests — Egypt no less than Saudi Arabia.

The relations of the Arab oil states of the Persian Gulf — chiefly Iraq and Saudi Arabia — with Egypt following the signing of the Camp David accords and the Baghdad meeting of foreign ministers of 1979 are also instructive in regard to this issue. Although the overriding response of most Arab states to Sadat's peacemaking move was one of rage, reflected in the decision made in Baghdad in March 1979 to ostracize Egypt from the community of Arab states by suspending its membership in the Arab League, breaking off diplomatic relations, and imposing an economic boycott,[28] the sanctions against Egypt were never fully enforced. Even if they had been enforced in the broad economic areas in which Egypt maintained ties with Arab countries — tourism, trade and private and public investment — they would have been insufficient in themselves to cause a real economic crisis, although they certainly would have hampered Egyptian economic development. Only in one way could the Arab oil states have dealt the Egyptian economy a severe blow: by shutting their doors to Egyptian migrant workers.

The number of Egyptian workers employed in the oil economies totalled about 1.5 million in 1979,[29] with official remittances to Egypt by these workers amounting to $2.2 billion that year.[30] The addition to this figure of the net increase of foreign currency deposits attributed to the remittances of migrant workers, and to remittances that found their way into Egypt through unofficial channels, brought the total contribution in foreign currency to the Egyptian economy to an even higher figure. However, even $2.2 billion, the figure ordinarily cited in Egyptian publications, represented a substantial contribution to Egypt's economy. Indeed, remittances had become a major income item in Egypt's current account since 1976, when they already totaled $755 million.[31]

Egyptian migrant workers were concentrated in four oil economies in the late 1970s: Saudi Arabia, Libya, Kuwait and the United Arab Emirates. Significantly, not only did this labor force not decline as a result of the decisions made at the Baghdad meeting of Arab leaders, it actually doubled over the two-year period following the signing of the Accords: by 1982, about three million Egyptian migrant workers were employed in the Arab oil economies, the principal increase having taken place in Iraq.[32] Concurrently, the flow of remittances increased, with total official remittances for the 1983/84 Egyptian fiscal year amounting to over $3.9 billion.[33] Unofficial estimates put this total at $5–$6 billion, which included remittances arriving both through official and unofficial channels, as well as the increase in personal foreign currency deposits and goods sent home by migrant workers.[34] Even the official figure of $3.9 billion reflected the substantial contribution of remittances to the Egyptian economy. In 1983/84 they were the most important item of foreign currency income, constituting 33 percent of total income from the export of goods and services ($11.8 billion), 76 percent of the trade deficit ($5.1 billion), and 13 percent of the GNP ($30 billion).[35]

Egyptian economic relations with other Arab states after 1979 remained on a normal footing in other important fields as well. Foreign currency deposits held in Egyptian banks in 1979 by both the Arab private and public sectors, amounting to roughly $4.0 billion, were not withdrawn, except for isolated instances.[36] There was no drop in tourism from countries such as Saudi Arabia, Kuwait and the United Arab Emirates, either. In fact, tourism from these countries increased between 1977 and 1984.[37] Even in terms of trade, the damage done to the Egyptian economy, when measured in absolute terms, was slight. Although exports of goods to all Arab states fell from a total of $161 million in 1978 to $88 million in 1980, they rose again to $126 million in 1981 and to $170 million in 1984.[38]

Undoubtedly, the Arab states that continued to maintain economic ties with Egypt had alternative options available in all the relevant fields, particularly in regard to the employment of migrant workers. Obviously, however, these alternatives were less desirable than the Egyptian option, whether for political, economic or social considerations. In other words, the economic relations maintained by Arab countries with Egypt were determined primarily by self-interest. Similarly, the viability of particularism proved to be decisively superior to that of Pan-Arabism. Especially striking in this regard is the fact that it was during the very years in which Egypt committed the most serious infraction in its history against the imperatives of Arab nationalism — a separate peace with Israel — that its economic ties with other Arab countries actually grew in scope and importance.

To conclude, during the oil decade the consolidation of the separate Arab nation-state received a considerable boost. The origin of this development was traced, at least in part, to the fact that while several Arab states were prospering, the social and economic problems of other Arab states became exacerbated as a result of the accelerated pace of population growth. Put another way: as the economic disparities grew, they assumed the guise of political differences that became increasingly more marked as time went on. This development also had its ideological manifestations in several Arab states, for example Egypt, Iraq and Saudi Arabia.

NOTES

1. *al-Ahram al-Iqtisadi*, 15 June 1979; Arab Republic of Egypt, CAPMAS, *SY 1952-1981*, Cairo: 1981; *Demographic Yearbook 1983*, p. 156.
2. D. MacKenzie, "Tackling Egypt's Baby Boom," *The Middle East*, October 1985, pp. 51-52; A. Charnock, "Simple Solution Saves Lives," ibid., December 1985, p. 54.
3. See, e.g., *al-Ahram*, 19 April 1987.
4. GDP growth rates in constant 1965 prices were: 0.6 percent in 1966, -1.2 in 1967, 1.6 in 1968, and 1.9 in 1972. See Khalid Ikram, *Egypt. Economic Management in a Period of Transition*, Baltimore and London: Johns Hopkins University Press, 1980, pp. 396–99, table 6 (hereafter: Ikram).
5. John Waterbury, *The Egypt of Nasser and Sadat*, Princeton: Princeton University Press, 1983, pp. 51-53.
6. For detailed data on the monetary reserves of the Arab oil countries in the years 1974-84, see OAPEC, *Secretary General's Eighth Annual Report 1981*, Kuwait: 1982, p. 66; IMF, *World Economic Outlook 1983*, Washington D.C.: 1983, p. 187; *PE*, June 1985, p. 196.
7. See, e.g., Haikal's article, *al-Ahram*, 18 October 1968; Nasser's address on the occasion of July Revolution Day, *al-Ahram*, 24 July 1969.
8. Heller and Safran, "The New Middle Class," pp. 29-34.
9. Al-Hegelan and Palmer's conclusion that the low level of salaries explains inadequate incentives for enhanced performance by the Saudi bureaucracy need not mean that Saudi nationals employed in the public sector do not identify with the Saudi state. See "Bureaucracy and Development in Saudi Arabia," *MEJ* 39 (1985): 48-68.
10. Kingdom of Saudi Arabia, Central Planning Organization, *Development Plan A.H. 1390 (1970-74)*: p. 81; Joseph Chamie (ed.), *Saudi Arabia Yearbook 1980-81*, Beirut: 1980, p. 266.
11. Kavoussi, "Economic Growth," pp. 71-78.
12. *al-Ahram*, 2 September 1967; *al-Hayat*, 31 August-2 September 1967.
13. See, e.g., Anouar Abdel-Malek, *Egypt: Military Society*, New York: Vintage Books, 1968, pp. 285-87.
14. On these and additional arguments, see *al-Ahram*, 30 January and 22 May 1975, 2, 14 May, 27 July 1979; *al-Ahram al-Iqtisadi*, 15 January 1980, pp. 6-9; M. El-Beheiry, "Egypt and OPEC," in R.A. Stone (ed.), *OPEC and the Middle East*, New York: 1977; Daniel Dishon, "Inter-Arab Relations," *MECS* 3 (1978-79): 231.
15. This figure includes all kinds of government-to-government aid (grants and loans). Most sources mentioned below do not give estimates regarding military and defense aid; *al-Nahar Arab Report and Memo*, 23 April 1979; Ikram, pp. 350-51; J. Wien, *Saudi-Egyptian Relations: The Political and Military Dimensions of Saudi Financial Flows to Egypt*, Santa Monica: RAND, 1980, pp. 47-60; *World Development Report 1981*, p. 165 table 16; OECD, *Aid from OPEC Countries*, Paris: 1983, table II.8; UNCTAD, *Trade and Development Report 1983*, New York: UN, 1983, pp. 61-76.
16. *al-Qabas*, 14 April 1979; ARAMCO, *World Magazine*, 1979, pp. 2-3. See also *MEED*, 6 April 1979.
17. Nazih Ayubi, "OPEC Surplus Funds and Third World Development: The Egyptian Case," *JSAMES* 4/4 (1982): 46 (hereafter: Ayubi).
18. OECD, *Aid from OPEC*, table II.8.
19. *The Middle East*, June 1979.
20. *al-Ahram*, 22 May 1975; *MENA*, 26 July 1976.
21. *MEED*, 7 May 1976, p. 17; Ikram, pp. 345-46, 364.
22. For details on the "food riots," see *al-Ahram*, 19–20 January 1977; *MEED*, 28 January 1977, pp. 5-6, 13.
23. Waterbury, *Nasser and Sadat*, p. 419.
24. Ikram, p. 351. OECD, *Aid from OPEC*, table II.8; *Ruz al-Yusuf*, no. 2652, 9

April 1979. In early August 1976 Sadat told delegations of Egyptian students in the U.S.: "The Arab aid fund [GODE], amounting to two billion [US dollars], is not sufficient. Our Arab brothers ought to appreciate our situation...they ought to reconsider this fund, because two billion is not enough." Radio Cairo, 3 August 1976.

25. Ayubi, pp. 54-55.
26. *al-Ahram*, 4 August 1976; also 3 April 1979.
27. John Waterbury, *Hydropolitics of the Nile Valley*, Syracuse: Syracuse University Press, 1979, pp. 172-73; Fouad Ajami, *The Arab Predicament*, Cambridge: Cambridge University Press, 1981, p. 103; Malcolm H. Kerr, "Introduction: Egypt in the Shadow of the Gulf," in Malcolm H. Kerr and El Sayed Yassin (eds.), *Rich and Poor States in the Middle East*, Boulder Colo.: Westview Press, 1982, pp. 9-10.
28. Avraham Sela, *Ahdut be-tokh perud ba-ma'arekhet ha-beyn 'arvit*, Jerusalem: Magnes Press, 1982, pp. 183-88.
29. *al-Ahram*, 18 September 1978.
30. WB, *World Tables*, vol. 1, *Economic Data*, Baltimore and London: 1984, p. 283.
31. Ibid.
32. *al-Ahram*, 5 August 1982, 13 August 1983, 12 October 1984.
33. *International Financial Statistics*, December 1985.
34. For data on personal foreign currency deposits, see National Bank of Egypt, *Economic Bulletin, 1982-1983*, various issues.
35. These calculations are based on IMF data. See *Direction of Trade Statistics, Yearbook 1985*, p. 163; IMF, *International Financial Statistics 1985*.
36. Ayubi, p. 54.
37. Government of Egypt, General Authority for the Promotion of Tourism, *Tourist Statistical Information, 1975-1984*, Cairo, 1985.
38. IMF, *Direction of Trade Statistics, Yearbook 1985*, p. 164.

5

The Expansion of Higher Education

INTRODUCTION

The oil decade gave rise to great expectations in the Arab societies in the Middle East for substantial and rapid changes in a wide range of areas — political, economic, social and cultural. In the 1980s, it became clear, however, that only few of these expectations had been realized. One such area was higher education.

Higher education in the Arab countries during the 1970s and 1980s saw a number of far-reaching changes, not only in size (quantitatively) but also in curricula and academic research (qualitatively). Each of these changes deserves a separate study, based on the appropriate categories of information and research methods. In this chapter I will examine quantitative changes only — qualitative changes may be studied on the basis of our results but they of course do not fall within the scope of the present inquiry.

Four basic groups of questions form the basis of this study:

(1) What were the changes in the number of students enrolled in institutions of higher education in Arab countries, and in the size of academic faculty? This leads to an additional question: What new universities were established in the Arab states?

(2) Was there, in parallel to the change in the number of enrolled students, also a change in the makeup of the student body according to demographic criteria and subjects studied? More specifically, was there a change in the proportion of students studying the exact sciences (including life sciences) and engineering?

(3) What changes occurred in the number of students who successfully completed their studies? What was the breakdown of these graduates according to areas of study? More specifically, what was the rate of change in the number of graduates in the exact sciences and engineering?

(4) Lastly, did changes in the number of enrolled students also lead to changes in the proportion of students in the relevant age groups and in the proportion of students in the general population in each of the countries included in this research?

Initially, my intention had been to examine several additional areas in which changes occurred, including changes in facilities, equipment and library collections, as well as changes in the amount of resources (regular budgets and development budgets) allocated to institutions of higher education. However, these issues could not be explored owing to insufficient data. In contrast to the areas outlined in the four groups of questions above, for which governments and universities supplied sufficient data (although even these data, as will be shown, have certain weaknesses), the available data published in the Arab states themselves or outside them regarding the physical development and the financial state of the institutions of higher education proved insufficient to serve as a basis for credible research.

The extent and quality of the data are also the factors that eventually determined which Arab states were included in the research. From the 1960s onward, only seven Arab states in the Middle East — Egypt, Iraq, Syria, Jordan, Saudi Arabia, Kuwait and the United Arab Emirates — published or made available to international research institutions data which are satisfactory quantitatively and qualitatively, and they form the basis of this study. The remaining Arab states did not, for various reasons, publish sufficient information, so that it was not possible to discuss them within the context of this work. Developments in higher education experienced by the Palestinians were not included in this study, since these have already been presented in a number of publications.[1]

The study presents developments that occurred over more than twenty years, from the late 1960s through the late 1980s. This period saw a great leap forward in the size of the higher education system in the Arab states. In a number of cases, where required for descriptive purposes or in order to analyze a particular development, earlier years are also discussed. While the 1970s and 1980s did not represent a unified unit concerning development of institutions of higher education, overall development trends justify addressing the topic in this periodic framework.

The study is macro-quantitative. Its purpose is to present the main developments of larger systems over time. The reader interested in the course of development of a certain university in the 1970s and 1980s should turn to more particularized studies that have been published, albeit limited in number.[2]

Three categories of primary sources were available: (1) annuals and catalogs published by universities in Arab countries, which sometimes included extensive data;[3] (2) statistical reports, annuals and other official publications by governmental bodies, such as central bureaus of statistics, education ministries, and official research organizations;[4] and (3) statistical annuals and information yearbooks published by inter-Arab and international organizations, especially the UNESCO statisticai yearbook.[5]

The use of these sources raised a number of problems. The first concerned the degree of statistical coverage of quantitative developments in systems of higher education. Not every university regularly published statistical yearbooks or other publicaiions containing information on university developments. For this reason, it was not possible to construct complete series of data reflecting developments in higher education based on these sources.

Inter-Arab and international organizations and agencies collected data beyond what can be found in university and government publications, with the data compiled by UNESCO apparently the most complete. However, even UNESCO, which has good access to centers of information in Arab countries, faced certain difficulties in gathering complete and up-to-date information. For example, the same figure often appears repeatedly in UNESCO yearbooks for the total number of enrolled students, year after year. That is, when data could not be updated, the yearbook gave the figure for the previous year, and sometimes for several years previously, without citing this practice.[6] This method is even more common in another publication, *The World of Learning* (*WOL*), published by Europa Publications, which sometimes repeats the same figures for students and academic staff in four or five successive issues, again without indicating the absence of updating.[7] Nevertheless, no alternative source to the UNESCO yearbook is available in terms of reliability of the aggregate data.

Another difficulty, significant because of its bearing on the quality of the data, lies in the differing definitions in the Arab countries for the variables examined by this study. For example, there is no agreed definition for the term "member of the academic staff": it can mean only those with full appointments in the regular academic track, or it can also include part-time appointments not in the regular track, such as external teachers, teaching assistants and the like. In addition, several of the official publications do not give any definition or explanation for the variables, in particular for those which involve an a priori difficulty in definition and measurement. Even when an agreed definition exists for an important variable, such as "university" or "enrolled student," there is no guarantee that the data provided in the official publications and even in the UNESCO yearbooks conform with this definition. For example, some of the data on "enrolled students" also include those studying in "open universities," and some do not.[8]

Given this situation, discussion of the aggregate data is restricted to areas for which the UNESCO yearbooks or other reliable publications provide data. For example, it was not possible to discuss the distribution of students according to level of studies (baccalaureate degree as compared with advanced degrees), since neither the UNESCO nor any other statistical yearbook provides complete data on this subject.[9]

QUANTITATIVE GROWTH

A. NUMBER OF ENROLLED STUDENTS

The 1970s and early 1980s were years of a great leap forward in the quantitative expansion of the system of higher education in the Arab world, with the number of students multiplying several times both in the "poor" and in the "rich" Arab states.

This process of quantitative expansion took place in two stages. The first began at the end of the 1960s or the beginning of the 1970s and continued until the middle of the decade, and was characterized by an unprecedented jump in the total number of students (male and female). To illustrate, the number of students in Egypt increased from 218,000 in 1970 to 462,000 in 1976, a growth of 244,000 students (112 percent) within six years. In absolute terms this was the greatest quantitative expansion in the Arab states since the establishment of universities there. The most rapid relative increase during this period was in Saudi Arabia, where the number of students enrolled in universities increased from 8,000 in 1970 to 44,000 in 1977, an increase of 450 percent within seven years. The total number of students in the seven Arab countries included in this study increased from 244,000 in 1970 to 711,000 in 1976–77, or an increase of 2.9 times within 6-7 years (see table 5.1).

The period between 1977 and 1985 marked the second stage of quantitative expansion, during which some of the Arab states recorded a slowing down in the rate of growth of student enrollment. Saudi Arabia and Kuwait merely doubled their student populations, the former from 44,000 in 1977 to 95,000 in 1984, and the latter from 12,000 in 1977 to 24,000 in 1986. In Egypt the rate of growth was lower still: from 462,000 in 1976 to 614,000 in 1984 — an increase of only 32.9 percent in eight years. Developments in Jordan and in the United Arab Emirates, however, were different: the rate of growth in student enrollment in these states during the second stage was similar to that in the first stage. In Jordan the number of students increased from 17,000 in 1977 to 61,000 in 1986 (a total increase of 259 percent), and in the United Arab Emirates from 519 to 7,640 during 1977–85 (an increase of 14.7 times). Thus, while expansion continued during the second stage, it was less uniform and varied from state to state. The total number of students in six of the Arab countries (Iraq did not publish data for 1986) increased from 620,000 in 1976–77 to 981,000 in 1986 — an increase of 58 percent, compared with an increase of 291 percent for the seven countries during 1970–76.

This expansion of the higher education system came to a gradual halt in 1985–86. The increase in the number of students was limited in both absolute and relative terms: in Jordan, from 61,000 in 1986 to 66,000 in 1988 (an increase of 9 percent), and in Saudi Arabia from 114,000 in 1986 to 127,000 in 1989 (an increase of 12 percent). In Egypt there was actually a decrease in absolute terms: from 614,000 in 1984 to 589,000 in 1987. An absolute decrease was also recorded in the United Arab Emirates: from 7,600 in 1985 to 7,400 in 1987 (see table 5.1).

A trend that actually exceeded the growth in total number of students was in the proportion of women enrolled at university. In Syria and Iraq this proportion increased from about 20 percent in 1970 (19 percent in Syria and 22 percent in Iraq) to 36 percent during 1986–88. An even more far-reaching change occurred in Saudi Arabia: the proportion of women at Saudi universities increased from very low rates of 4 percent in 1965 and 8 percent in 1970 to 39 percent in 1986. In Jordan, Kuwait and the United Arab

Table 5.1
Seven Arab countries: total students enrolled[a] in universities[b], 1965-88
(various years)

	Egypt	Syria	Iraq	Jordan	Saudi Arabia	Kuwait	UAE
1965	175,254	32,653	28,377	4,049f	3,625	418	—
1970	218,278	40,896	48,994e	4,518	8,492	2,686	—
1977	462,328c	83,260c	91,358c	17,219	43,897	12,391	519
1980	528,751	140,180	103,176	36,549	62,074	13,630	2,734
1986	592,256	182,933	..	60,553	113,529	24,384	7,640g
1988	589,111d	..	130,278	65,979	..	25,521d	..

Notes:
a Including advanced degrees.
b Institutions of higher education that grant academic degrees.
c Figure for 1976.
d Figure for 1987.
e Figure for 1971.
f Figure for 1966.
g Figure for 1985.

Source:
UNESCO, SY, volumes for 1967-91.

Figure 5.1
*Seven Arab countries: total students enrolled in universities,
1965-88 (various years)*

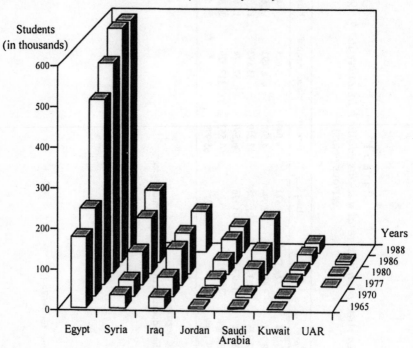

Notes and source: table 5.1

Emirates, by contrast, the rate of women was already relatively high by the 1970s, and toward the end of the 1980s women represented half or more of the total number of students in these three countries. Only in Egypt was there merely a relatively modest increase in the rate of women in the student population, from 27 percent in 1970 to 35 percent in 1987 (see table 5.2). All in all, the leap in the total number of women students enrolled in universities in the Arab countries under discussion (with the exception of Iraq) during a 16-year period is impressive: from 69,000 in 1970 to 360,000 in 1986, or 522 percent (see table 5.2).

Another significant quantitative change concerns the division of the student population according to areas of study, or, more precisely, according to the faculties in which they were enrolled. In most of the countries examined, the number of students studying sciences and engineering increased at a greater rate than the overall increase in the student population. The sharpest development in this area was in Syria, where the rate of students studying in these faculties increased by 39 percent in 1980 and by 42 percent in 1986. In absolute terms this represented an increase from 4,994 students in 1965 to 77,146 students in 1986. While the rate of growth in Syria was particularly high, an increase in the proportion of students in sciences and engineering was also recorded in Jordan, Saudi Arabia and Kuwait during the period under study. The increase in absolute terms was particularly obvious, since in the countries in question only a few thousand students were enrolled at these faculties in the early 1970s. In Egypt, however, the process was different. The proportion of engineering and science students dropped in the early stages of the accelerated quantitative increase in the student population, a trend that continued until the late 1980s. In 1970 the proportion of students in these fields in Egypt reached 35 percent, while in 1980 it fell to 26 percent and in 1987 to 21 percent. In absolute terms the number of students enrolled in the engineering and science faculties was lower at the end of the 1980s than in the period from 1975 to 1985: in 1975, 58,000 students were enrolled in these faculties, while in 1987 this number was only 49,000. With the exception of Egypt, however, there was a large overall increase in the number of students enrolled in the science and engineering faculties in the Arab states under review. While in 1970 the total was about 107,000, in 1986–88 it was 298,000 (see table 5.3).

The overall growth in the number of students enrolled in colleges and universities was reflected in a significant rise in the proportion

Table 5.2

Seven Arab countries: women students enrolled[a] in universities[b], 1965-88
(various years) (percentage of total students enrolled)

	Egypt	Syria	Iraq	Jordan	Saudi Arabia	Kuwait	UAE
1965	20.9	16.8	26.9	29.6[f]	3.3	42.1	—
1970	26.5	18.8	21.6[e]	29.9	8.1	48.4	—
1977	30.4[c]	24.9[c]	32.0[c]	37.0	20.9	53.6	39.5
1980	31.8	29.3	29.6	45.6	27.9	57.3	47.8
1986	34.3	35.5	..	47.9	39.4	54.6	58.1[g]
1988	34.5[d]	..	35.5	49.5	..	54.7[d]	..

Notes:

a Including advanced degrees.
b Institutions of higher education that grant academic degrees.
c Figure for 1976.
d Figure for 1987.
e Figure for 1971.
f Figure for 1966.
g Figure for 1985.

Source:
UNESCO, *SY*, volumes for 1967-91.

of men and women students aged 20-24 (the age group embracing most students in institutions of higher education). The proportion of study in institutions of higher education in Egypt and Syria jumped from 7 and 8 percent respectively in 1965 to 20 and 18 percent in 1986. In Jordan and in the oil countries of the Arabian Peninsula the proportions in 1965 were smaller than in Egypt, so that the relative change was greater: in Jordan from 2 percent in 1965 to 27 percent in 1980, and in Saudi Arabia and Kuwait from 1-2 percent in 1965 to 13 and 16 percent respectively in 1986. As in other surveys, here too the proportions for Saudi Arabia are deflated because of an upward tilt in the size of the total population in that country. Overall, the proportion of study in institutions of higher education in Arab countries in the latter half of the 1980s in the above-mentioned age groups was around 20 percent (see table 5.4). Compared with one or two out of every 100 young people aged 20-24 who studied at an institution of higher education in the mid-1960s, one out of every five was enrolled at the end of the 1980s. Enrollment rates were higher in the male population than in the female population in all the countries examined.

Significantly, during the years of rapid growth of the system of higher education, the rates of increase of student enrollment exceeded the overall natural increase rates, which themselves were very high (2.5–3.5 percent annually).[10] This development was reflected in the ratio of the number of students in institutions of higher education per 100,000 inhabitants: growth in this ratio was recorded for 1970–85 in all the countries included in this study. The growth in Jordan was especially impressive (from 657 students per 100,000 inhabitants in 1975 to 1,992 students in 1985). Jordan had the highest student:population ratio of all the countries in the mid-1980s, overtaking Egypt, which had held this record until then (see table 5.5).

B. NUMBER OF FACULTY MEMBERS

Obviously, such substantial growth in the number of students in all the countries under review necessitated a rapid rise in the number of faculty members. Indeed, available data show impressive growth in these figures. However, as noted above, the data on staff members are even more problematic than those relating to other areas connected with the quantitative development of systems of

Table 5.3

Seven Arab countries: students enrolled[a] in faculties of sciences and engineering[b], 1965-88 (various years) (percentage of total students enrolled)

	Egypt	Syria	Iraq	Jordan	Saudi Arabia	Kuwait	UAE
1965	32.3	15.3	36.3	13.6	12.1	—	—
1970	34.5	31.6	34.3	..	20.1	—	—
1975	27.6	35.5	40.0	22.7	18.0	24.1	—
1980	26.3	38.9	40.2	22.6	18.3	29.2	15.1
1985	22.0[c]	42.5[e]	..	32.9[c]	23.2[c]	29.6[e]	12.9
1988	21.2[d]	42.2[c]	32.0	29.4	21.8[c]	35.1[d]	15.7[d]

Notes:

a Including advanced degrees.

b In academic institutions only.

c Figure for 1986.

d Figure for 1987.

e Figure for 1984.

Source:

UNESCO, SY, volumes for 1967-91.

Table 5.4

Seven Arab countries: gross enrollment rates in post-secondary educational institutions[a], 1965–87 (various years, ages 20–24)

	Egypt	Syria	Iraq	Jordan	Saudi Arabia	Kuwait	UAE
1965	6.8	8.0	4.1	1.8	0.6	—	—
1970	7.9	8.3	5.2	2.2	1.3	3.6	—
1975	13.5	12.1	9.0	..	4.1	9.0	—
1980	17.7	17.6	9.3	26.6	7.3	10.8	2.3
1985	20.3	18.7	12.4	..	10.9	15.8	8.7
1987	20.0	..	12.5	..	13.4	16.6	8.7

Notes:
a Including institutions that do not grant academic degrees.

Source:
UNESCO, *SY*, volumes for 1977-89.

Table 5.5

Seven Arab countries: number of students in post-secondary educational institutions[a],
per 100,000 inhabitants, 1970-85

(various years)

	Egypt	Syria	Iraq	Jordan	Saudi Arabia	Kuwait	UAE
1970	711	682	454	197	137	361	—
1975	1,323	990	781	657	364	804	—
1980	1,751	1,611	820	1,647	662	991	282
1985	1,837	1,734	1,108	1,992	917	1,377	576

Note:
a Including institutions that do not grant academic degrees.

Source:
UNESCO, *SY*, volumes for 1980 and 1989.

higher education in the Arab countries, and conclusions based on them would be of doubtful value.

The first difficulty is inherent in the absence of categorization within the data as to job status and academic rank. For example, it is unclear from the explanatory matter, where present, whether the data on number of staff members include only teachers holding full positions or in fact the entire teaching staff, including part-time positions, teachers employed on an hourly basis and others. Furthermore, the published data omit grouping the staff according to academic rank, which has important implications. For example, the Egyptian universities grade a large proportion of master's students (holders of a B.A.) as assistants, albeit with a minuscule salary, whose primary task is to lighten the senior lecturer's teaching load.[11] The data on academic staff in Egypt appear to include this rank and position. The second difficulty is inherent in the great variation between the data themselves, especially the difference between UNESCO data and those in yearbooks published by countries and universities, as well as the *WOL* volumes. Unfortunately, there is no way to establish which set of data is more credible. The third difficulty is inherent in the incompleteness of the data regarding all members of academic staffs in the countries under discussion. In some cases, data are absent entirely, sometimes for periods of many years.

Nevertheless, a study of the series of data published in the UNESCO yearbooks produces the following picture. In Egypt, the total number of faculty members rose from approximately 12,000 in 1970 to approximately 30,000 in 1985, or a growth of 2.5 times. While the total number of faculty members in all the other countries was smaller, growth rates during this period were higher than in Egypt. In Syria, the total number of staff members grew from approximately 1,000 in 1970 to approximately 4,500 in 1985, or a growth of 4.3 times. Kuwait showed similar growth — 4.5 times. While Jordan experienced even higher growth rates, Saudi Arabia showed the highest growth: the former from 344 to 1,295 staff members, a growth of 7.7 times; the latter from 697 to over 9,000, a growth of 13.3 times during 1970-85 (see table 5.6).

Because of the problematic nature and quality of the data on faculty size, there is limited significance to an analysis of the changes that occurred in the student:faculty ratio. This reservation notwithstanding, it is nevertheless apparent that the rate of growth of academic staff was slower than that of number of students during 1970–85 in Egypt, Jordan and Kuwait, while in Saudi Arabia and Syria these rates closely paralleled each other and were possibly even higher for academic staff (see table 5.6).

The alternative series of data derived form the statistical yearbooks issued by the countries themselves, the university yearbooks and the *WOL* yearbooks differ considerably in terms of number of academic staff members in Syria and in Saudi Arabia (see table 5.6). These data tend to reinforce the conclusion that the growth rate of academic staff members, regardless of rank, was similar to, or even exceeded, the growth rate of students during 1970–85. Regarding the studentlecturer ratio, both sets of data point to a low ratio, with the lowest of all the countries researched in Saudi Arabia — between 11:1 and 12:1 during the period under discussion. Both sets of data also indicate that Syria had a very high ratio during the early 1970s — between 36:1 and 38:1, although this dropped during the mid-1980s to between 26:1 and 30:1. The student:lecturer ratio appeared to have worsened in Jordan and Kuwait — in Jordan from 15:1 to 21:1, or, according to other data, to 41:1, and in Kuwait from 24:1 to 28:1. Only in the case of Egypt is there a significant divergence between the two sets of data, with the UNESCO data indicating a worsened ratio and the alternative data showing an improved ratio. In any case, Egypt', ratios for the 1980s vary from 21:1 to 29:1.

C. NUMBER OF UNIVERSITY GRADUATES (DEGREE RECIPIENTS)

As would be expected, the growth in student enrollment in universities led to a rise in number of graduates, that is, recipients of academic degrees. The total number of degree recipients (baccalaureates and advanced degrees) in all institutions of higher education grew from approximately 45,000 in 1970 to approximately 169,000 in 1985 (see table 5.7). Egypt stood out in growth of number of degree recipients in absolute terms: from approximately 31,000 in 1970 to approximately 117,000 in 1985. Saudi Arabia made the largest jump in relative terms: from 833 graduates in 1970 to 13,000 in 1985 — a growth rate of 16.2 times. Both Jordan and Syria also showed impressive growth absolutely and relatively in number of graduates from institutions of higher education during 1970–85, the former from approximately 1,400 to 15,000, the latter from approximately 3,400 to 19,000 graduates.

The development in the number of engineering-degree recipients is of particular interest. In 1970, only Egypt and Iraq trained significant numbers of engineers — over 5,000 in Egypt and some

Table 5.6

Seven Arab countries: teaching staff[a] in institutions of higher education[b], 1965-88
(various years)

	Egypt	Syria	Iraq	Jordan	Saudi Arabia	Kuwait	UAE
1965	..	839	1,455	75	278	—	—
1970	11,859	1,037	1,822	168	697	189	—
1975	..	1,332	2,965	344	2,133	327	
1980	..	..	4,627	..	6,598	608	208
1985	29,889	4,504	..	1,295	9,297	858	449[d]
1988	..	..	..	..	..	1,140[c]	460[c]

Notes:
a Holders of full- or part-time academic appointments in varied employment tracks in institutions of higher education.
b Universities and other institutions that grant academic degrees and/or diplomas.
c Figure for 1987.
d Figure for 1984.

Source:
UNESCO, *SY*, 1977 and 1989.

Table 5.7

Seven Arab countries: university graduates[a], 1965-85
(various years)

	Egypt	Syria	Iraq	Jordan	Saudi Arabia	Kuwait	UAE
1965	21,239	2,464	2,349[b]	623	524	—	—
1970	30,905	3,404	7,779	1,379	833	369	—
1975	53,162	5,170	17,658	6,519[d]	3,088[d]	1,187[e]	—
1980	80,443	16,625	22,486[c]	7,326	8,188	2,593	568
1985	116,854	19,384	..	15,186	13,083	2,038	2,337

Notes:

a Including advanced degrees.
b Figure for 1964.
c Figure for 1979.
d Figure for 1976.
e Figure for 1974.

Source:
UNESCO, *SY*, 1969 and 1989.

Figure 5.2
*Seven Arab countries: university graduates,
1965-85 (various years)*

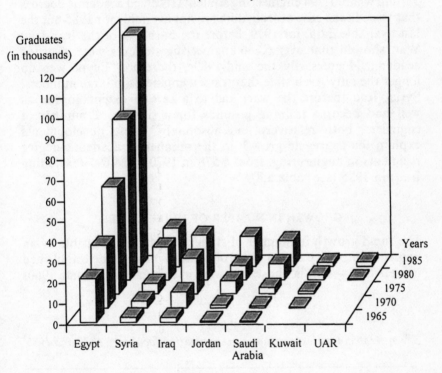

Notes and source: table 5.7

1,180 in Iraq — while the number of graduates in this field in the other countries under review was relatively low — between 223 in Syria and 32 in Jordan that year. By the mid-1980s, however, the number of graduates had risen remarkably in most of the countries. Egypt showed the most significant rise in absolute terms: over 10,000 engineering students completed their studies successfully and were awarded academic degrees. In relative terms, Syria and Jordan showed the most impressive growth, with 5,568 academically trained engineers joining the work force in Syria in 1985, and an even more impressive measure of relative growth in Jordan where 1,794 engineering students received academic degrees that year. In the case of Iraq, data are not available for 1985 but the last available data, for 1979, before the outbreak of the Iran-Iraq War, showed that over 6,200 engineering students were awarded academic degrees. By the mid-1980s, therefore, Egypt was no longer the only Arab state that trained engineers in large numbers. Syria, Iraq (before the war) and to a certain extent Jordan as well had become training grounds for a significant number of engineers, both relatively and absolutely. These developments explain the aggregate growth in the number of academic-degree recipients in engineering, from 6,578 in 1970 to 24,691 (excluding Iraq) in 1985 (see table 5.8).

GROWTH IN NUMBER OF UNIVERSITIES

The rapid growth in number of students was made possible by an unprecedented expansion in enrollment in most of the established universities — that is, those that were in existence in the late 1960s

Table 5.8

Seven Arab countries: graduates in engineering faculties[a], 1970 and 1985

	Egypt	Syria	Iraq	Jordan	Saudi Arabia	Kuwait	UAE
1970	5,071	223	1,180	32	34	38	—
1985	10,023	5,568	..	1,794	862	168	43

Note:

a Including advanced degrees.

Source:

UNESCO, *SY*, 1972 and 1987.

— as well as by the founding of new universities, which had tens of thousands of students enrolled within a few years of their opening (see table 5.9).

In Egypt, the number of students at the established universities of 'Ayn Shams, Cairo, al-Azhar and Alexandria was particularly noteworthy: during the mid-1980s, when enrollment reached a peak, each of these universities had 90,000–120,000 students. These institutions became, and remained, the largest in terms of enrollment in the entire Arab world. In addition, seven new universities opened in Egypt during a five-year period (1972–76): the universities of Mansura (1972), Tanta and Zaqaziq (1974), Hilwan (1975), Minya, Manufiyya and Suez Canal (1976). An effort was made, with the establishment of these institutions, to decentralize the higher education system and curtail the tremendous pressure exerted by potential students on the established universities in Cairo and Alexandria. Noteworthy among the new universities was the exceptional growth in enrollment at Zaqaziq University: in 1984, ten years after it opened, it had an enrollment of some 70,000 students (for all degrees). Mansura and Tanta universities also became large institutions, each with an enrollment of 40,000–45,000 students in the mid-1980s. From then onward, as noted above, not only did the quantitative growth in most Egyptian universities slow down, but a drop in student enrollment in absolute terms was also recorded. This development resulted from government policy aimed at reducing the size of the student population and the pool of university graduates owing to the inability of the Egyptian economy to absorb the growing academically trained sector.

As in Egypt, the growth in the number of students in Syria was divided between the established and the new universities, with the established institutions attracting the larger proportion. Damascus University had some 82,000 students at the end of the 1980s, while Halab University had approximately 51,000 students. Two new universities were established in peripheral areas during the 1970s: Tishrin in Ladhiqiyya (1971), which had some 18,000 students in 1988, and al-Ba'th in Homs (1979), which had approximately 13,000 students that year.

Iraq had only one university until the 1960s, Baghdad University, consisting of a group of 14 colleges — the first of which, the Law College, was founded in 1908 — which were combined in 1958 to form a single university. Baghdad University had an enrollment of some 19,000 on the eve of the Iran-Iraq War.

Table 5.9

Seven Arab countries: universities by number of students enrolled and academic staff members, the 1980s

University	Location	Year of founding	Update year	Number of students enrolled	Number of academic staff members
EGYPT					
al-Azhar	Cairo	970	1988/89	130,000	:
'Ayn Shams	Cairo	1950	1985/86	100,179	4,703
Alexandria	Alexandria	1942	1982/83	92,000	3,610
Cairo	Cairo	1908	1987/88	76,794	4,494
Zaqaziq	Zaqaziq	1974	1988/89	64,908	4,331
Asyut	Asyut	1957	1984/85	46,600	2,225
Tanta	Tanta	1972	1984/85	40,121	1,482
Mansura	Mansura	1972	1988/89	36,047	1,215
Hilwan	Hilwan	1975	1988/89	31,352	1,281
Manufiyya	Manufiyya	1976	1985/86	18,366	863
Minya	Minya	1976	1982/83	16,120	770
Suez Canal	Isma'iliyya	1976	1988/89	11,991	1,050
SYRIA					
Damascus	Damascus	1903	1988/89	81,175	2,609
Halab	Halab	1960	1988/89	50,738	1,995
Tishrin	Ladhiqiyya	1971	1986/87	18,130	214
al-Ba'th	Homs	1979	1988/89	12,860	183
IRAQ					
Mosul	Mosul	1967	1986/87	21,471	1,400
Baghdad	Baghdad	1957	1979/80	19,300	1,500
Basra	Basra	1964	1984/85	13,600	616

94

al-Mustansiriyya	Baghdad	1963	1988/89	18,000	734
Technological	Baghdad	1975	1984/85	7,384	269
Salah al-Din	Irbil	1968	1987/88	7,000	560
JORDAN					
al-Urdun	Amman	1962	1987/88	15,609	795
Yarmuk	Irbid	1976	1985/86	11,500	470
Mu'ta	Karak	1981	1987/88	3,000	70
SAUDI ARABIA					
King Sa'ud	Riyadh	1957	1987/88	32,000	2,730
King 'Abd al-'Aziz	Jiddah	1967	1986/87	20,077	1,147
Umm al-Qura	Mecca	1979	1987/88	14,972	1,172
King Fahd	Dhahran	1963	1984/85	4,500	780
King Faysal	Dammam	1969	1985/86	3,660	485
KUWAIT					
Kuwait	Kuwait City	1962	1988/89	12,500	955
UAE					
United Arab Enirates	al-'Ayn	1976	1988/89	8,000	583

Notes:
a Universities that had an enrollment of 3,000 students or more during the update year.
b Latest acceptable update in the sources listed below.

Sources:
Selected volums of the following yearbooks for 1981-91: *WOL, International Handbook of Universities, al-Dalil al-'amm lil jama'at al-'arabiyya.*

Figure 5.3

Seven Arab countries: universities by number of students enrolled, the 1980s

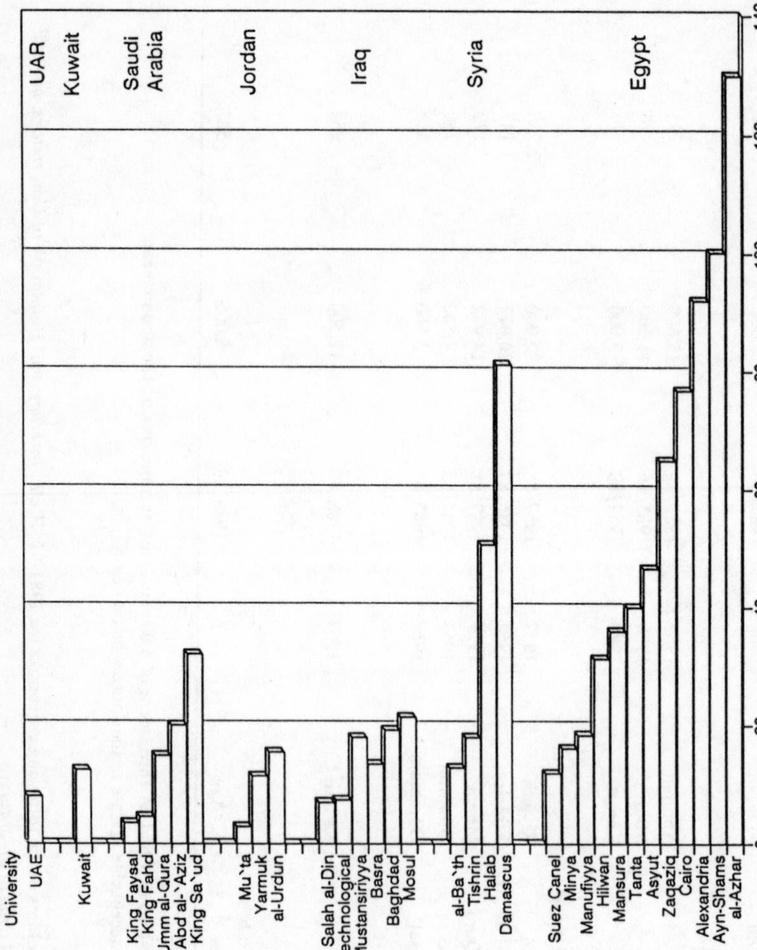

Source: table 5.9

Three new universities were established in peripheral areas during the 1960s: Basra (1964), Mosul (1967) and Salah al-Din at Irbil (1968). An additional university in Baghdad, al-Mustansariyya, was inaugurated in 1963. Based on partial data on higher education in Iraq since the outbreak of the Iran-Iraq War, it would appear that Mosul and al-Mustansiriyya universities had some 20,000 students each in the late 1980s.

Jordan was one of a group of countries in which universities were first established only after the Second World War. Jordan's two major universities were founded in the 1960s and 1970s. The first and larger, al-Urdun University in Amman (1962), had an enrollment of some 16,000 in the late 1980s, while the second, Yarmuk University in Irbid (1976), had an enrollment of some 12,000 in 1988.

A characteristic of the two oil countries under review — Saudi Arabia and Kuwait — was that the growth in number of students during the 1970s and 1980s did not involve the establishment of new universities but rather the expansion of existing ones, mostly founded in the 1960s before the dramatic rise in oil prices and the advent of the oil decade. Three large universities functioned in Saudi Arabia in the late 1980s: King Sa'ud in Riyadh (1957), which had 32,000 students in 1987–88; 'Abd al-'Aziz in Jidda (1967) with some 21,000 students in 1986–87; and Umm al-Qura in Mecca (reorganized in 1979) with some 15,000 students in 1987–88. Kuwait had one university, Kuwait University (1962), with 12,500 students in 1988–89. The only new university established in the 1970s in the Arabian Peninsula was the United Arab Emirates University in al-'Ayn (1976), which had 8,000 students in 1988–89.

To summarize, during the late 1980s, thirty universities functioned in the Arab countries included in this study. Of them, two universities had 100,000 or more students each; five had 50,000–99,000 students each; seven had 20,000–49,000 students each; twelve had 10,000–19,000 students each; and the remaining four had 5,000–9,000 students each. Most of the universities were relatively young, the majority founded in the 1960s and 1970s. Of the thirty universities, only eight were in existence in the late 1950s. Nine new universities were inaugurated in the 1960s, and thirteen additional universities opened in the 1970s. Notably, no university has been established since 1980. Lastly, of the universities that functioned in the Arab countries in the late 1950s, only one (Asyut) was located in a peripheral area; the vast majority were situated in capitals and other major urban centers. By contrast, in the late 1980s, over half the universities (16 out of 30) were located outside metropolitan centers.

THE ORIGINS OF EXPANSION

The large-scale quantitative expansion of the systems of higher education in the Arab countries resulted from policies applied during a period of over two decades. Both the countries termed "progressive" — Egypt, Syria and Iraq — in which the middle class removed the traditional elite from power, and the "conservative" countries, such as Saudi Arabia and Jordan, where the monarchical elites were able to retain their position, allocated an increasing amount of resources for the development and maintenance of large-scale systems of higher education. Significantly, the contribution of the private sector to the quantitative expansion of the systems of higher education in the Arab countries during the period under review was marginal.

A commitment to processes of social modernization was common to both groups of countries. The ruling elites adopted the approach that the provision of education to the masses and the expansion of the secondary and higher educational systems were essential preconditions for change, namely social and economic modernization.[12]

Another important factor that raised the priority of the development of higher education as a national goal in the army officers' regimes was the desire of the rulers to broaden their political base, especially within the salaried middle class. The widening out of opportunities for higher education, involving only a small financial outlay on the part of those admitted to university, was intended to significantly expand the ranks of the middle class and widen the range of its social mobility. The assumption made by the leaders of these regimes was that this policy would ensure the support of the middle class for the domestic and foreign policies they adopted.

Although the general adherence in the oil states to traditional norms did not encourage comprehensive social modernization, the elites of these countries nevertheless followed the lead of the other Arab rulers in all that pertained to the development of educational systems generally and higher education in particular. The policy of accelerated economic development adopted by Saudi Arabia and Kuwait, for example, involved wide-ranging investment in developing human resources, including the expansion of institutions of higher education.

Another factor that pushed the governments of both the oil and the non-oil countries toward the development of higher education and motivated them to allocate significant resources to it was the 1967 war. The collapse of the Arab armies during the war was attributed in the Arab world to the existence of a wide educational and technological gap between Israel and the Arab states. The drive to close or at least narrow that gap was one of the factors that motivated Arab governments — certainly in the countries that were involved in the military confrontations with Israel, but also in the other Arab countries — to give high priority to the development of higher education.

Lastly, the growth in revenues in the oil states from the export of this raw material during 1973–82 was an important factor in promoting the goals established by the elites in the area of higher education. Not only did income from oil export finance the expansion of higher education in the oil states, it also led to growth in income in the "transit states" — Egypt, Syria and Jordan — thereby contributing to increased investment in universities in those states as well. A clear reflection of the policy of encouraging rapid growth in the university-trained population was the sole requirement of a high school matriculation certificate (or a comparable diploma) for admission to most university faculties. Moreover, tuition was waived in all the countries under review.[13] It is not surprising, therefore, that a growing number of young people, both men and women, sought higher education.

The slowdown in student growth rates in Egypt during the early 1980s and in most of the other Arab countries during the late 1980s was also a result of government policy. Two factors prompted the authorities to curb the growth of the student population. First, the rapid rise in number of graduates was not accompanied by a parallel rise in employment opportunities in some of the countries under discussion. The pace of economic growth was unable to accommodate this university-trained population, with the result that pockets of open and hidden unemployment were soon created. This development was discernible in Egypt as early as the 1970s, and in the other countries in the 1980s.[14] Second, the Arab states underwent an economic depression around the mid-1980s that lasted until the end of the decade. Brought on, among other things, by the sharp drop in income from oil exports, this depression began in 1983 and worsened during

1985–87. Not only did it affect economic activity in the oil states, it was also felt in the transit states. Its effect on the expansion of higher education was twofold: resources allocated by governments to development in this area were sharply reduced, while employment opportunities for the thousands of graduates who had begun their studies during the peak years of economic prosperity but graduated during the depression shrank. This led to a growing number of unemployed university graduates during the second half of the 1980s. Intra-regional migration was not an effective solution in those years. Furthermore, governments that had adopted a policy of accelerated expansion of higher education systems found themselves under threat, as young unemployed university graduates soon gravitated toward opposition parties and movements, some of them radical and illegal. In addition, pressure by International Monetary Fund and World Bank experts was brought to bear on the governments that were in difficult economic straits to cut back on budget allocations for higher education.[15] Against this background, the authorities began to constrict university entrance, both by administrative measures and by admission examinations. The results of this change in policy were evident in freezes or cutbacks in university development and a decrease in growth rates of the student population during the 1980s.

THE EFFECTS OF GROWTH

The expansion of the systems of higher education in the Arab countries had immediate social and economic effects. First, it widened the potential for social mobility. In countries where channels for social mobility during the 1950s and 1960s were limited to the military track, and to a lesser extent the bureaucratic track, the rapid expansion of the universities, combined with the absence of tuition fees, offered the opportunity to many thousands of young people from the lower classes both in cities and villages to raise their social status and join the middle class. However, it should be noted that broadening the channels of social mobility in fact reduced, at least in the short run, the benefits accruing to university graduates because of the glut of university graduates in the societies under discussion.

The rapid growth in the number of university graduates in countries where the system of higher education was already relatively developed by the early 1970s was one of the important factors in facilitating horizontal mobility within the Middle East, that is, the migration of graduates from one Arab economy to another, especially from Egypt to the Arab oil economies in the Persian Gulf.[16]

The growth in the relative share of academically trained persons employed in public and private education systems, government offices and the military led to a rise in average level of formal education of teachers, government officials and army officers in the countries under review. However, with the rise in number of university graduates, the public services became the major employers of this work force, resulting in high rates of hidden unemployment during the 1970s and 1980s.

The growth in number of recipients of baccalaureate and advanced degrees in the faculties of engineering, exact sciences and social sciences was one of the important factors in promoting the development of both veteran industries (food, textiles, wood and others) and new industries (petrochemicals), as well as a number of service branches (especially banking and tourism). Moreover, the rapid growth in the number of graduates in these fields allowed for a reduction, in relative terms — and in several economic branches in absolute terms as well — in the number of non-Arab university-trained workers, primarily from Europe and North America, who were employed in these economies.[17]

Of special importance in the realm of possible long-range effects on the societies involved was the dramatic growth in the number of women who attained higher education in the 1970s and 1980s. The strong connection between women's fertility and their level of education (fertility rates for women with secondary school education and higher are lower than those for women with partial secondary school education or less), a connection which is not dependent on other variables which also affect women's fertility rates, was borne out in the countries under discussion. The growth in absolute terms of the number of women enrolled in institutions of higher education during the 1970s and 1980s, together with the even greater growth, in absolute terms, of their number among high school graduates, were already reflected in a drop in fertility rates in the societies under review.[18] It is reasonable to assume that the influence of the education factor on fertility rates in these Arab societies will be of even greater significance in coming decades.

NOTES

1. Antony Thrall Sullivan, *Palestinian Universities under Occupation, Cairo Papers in Social Science* 11/2 (1988); Zivit Steinboim and Yona Bargur, *Koah adam aqademi ba-gadah ha-ma'aravit u-ve-hevel 'azza*, Tel Aviv: Armand Hammer Fund, 1991.
2. See, for example, Bayard Dodge, *Al-Azhar: A Millenium of Muslim Learning*, Washington D.C.: The Middle East Institute, 1961; Khalid Ali Mansour, *University in Transition. A Study in Institutional Development: A Case Study of Umm al-Qura University, Mecca, Saudi Arabia*, Unpublished Ed.D. Dissertation, Indiana University, 1983; Lawrence R. Myrphy, *The American University in Cairo: 1919-1987*, New York: Columbia University Press, 1987; Donald Malcolm Reid, *Cairo University and the Making of Modern Eqypt*, Cambridge: Cambridge University Press, 1990.
3. See, for example, Jama'at al-malik Sa'ud, *Dalil, 1407-1409*, Riyadh; *Statistical Yearbook 1988-1989*, Amman, 1989.
4. al-Jumhuriyya al-'Arabiyya al-Suriyya, al-Maktab al-markazi lil-ihsa', *al-Majmu'a li-'amm 1983... 1989*, Damascus, 1983... 1989; Arab Republic of Egypt, National Center for Educational Research, *Development of Education in the Arab Republic of Egypt 1985-1986*, Cairo, 1986 (herafter: *Education in Egypt*); Arab Republic of Egupt, CAPMAS, *SY 1952-1988*, Cairo, 1989; Hashemite Kingdom of Jordan, *Annual Statistical Report on Higher Education in Jordan, 1983-1984*, Amman, 1984; Kingdom of Saudi Arabia, Ministry of Education, *Development of Education in the Kingdom of Saudi Arabia, 1408-1410 A.H. / 1988-1990 A.D.*, Riyadh, 1410/1990.
5. Ittihad al-jama'at al-'arabiyya, al-Imana al-'amma, *al-Dalil al-'amm lil-jama'at al-'arabiyya*, Ist ed., Amman, 1988; The International Association of Universities, *International Handbook of Universities, 1969, 1978, 1983, 1986*, Paris, 1969... 1986; Europa Publications, *The World of Learning, 1966, 1971... 1990*, London, 1967... 1991 (hereafter: *WOL*); UNESCO, *SY 1965... 1991*, Paris, 1965-1991.
6. See and compare UNESCO, *SY 1989*, pp. 3-300, 3-343 and *1990*, p. 00.
7. See and compare, *WOL 1971-72*, p. 1356 and *1990*, p. 420; *1979-80*, p. 691 and *1989*, p. 716.
8. See and compare UNESCO, *SY 1989*, pp. 3-254 and 3-300.
9. See below, pp. 89 and 92.
10. WB, *World Tables*, 3rd ed., vol. 2 — *Social Data*, Baltimore and London: Johns Hopkins University Press, 1983, pp. 28, 45, 49, 87, 105, 109, 110. UN, ESCWA, *Statistical Abstract of the Region of the Economic and Social Commission for Western Asia 1981-1990*, Amman: UN, 1992, pp. 33, 73, 112, 162, 324, 366.
11. *Education in Egypt, 1984/85-1985/86*, p. 140; Samuel Klausner, "A Professor's-Eye View of the Egyptian Academy," *JHE* 57/4 (1986): 351, 359.
12. *Education in Egypt, 1981/82 to 1983/84*, pp. 4-5, 12-13; Hashemite Kingdam of Jordan, Ministry of Education, *Five Year Educational Plan, 1982-1985*, Amman: MOE, 1981, pp. 22, 40-41; Mohammed Ahmed Rasheed, "Education as an Instrument of Progress in the Arab Gulf States," in M.S. El-Azhary (ed.), *The Impact of Oil Revenues on Arab Gulf Development*, London and Sydney: Croom Helm, 1984, pp. 180-81.
13. Bikas C. Sanyal et al., *University Education and the Labour Market in the Arab Republic of Egypt*, Oxford: Pergamon Press, 1982, p. 104; Byron G. Massialas and Samir Ahmed Jarrar, *Education in the Arab World*, New York: Praeger, 1983, p. 215.
14. *al-Ahali*, 4 March 1987; *al-Ahram al-Iqtisadi*, 18 January 1988, and 28 May 1990; *Ruz al-Yusuf*, 24 July 1989; *Emirates News*, 21 May 1986; *al-Yamama*, 12 November 1986; *'Ukaz*, 23 November 1986; *al-Ra'y*, 29 May 1989; *Jordan Times*, 14 May 1990.
15. Ikram, pp. 129, 136-37, 326-27.
16. Nader Fargany, "Differentials in Labour Migration in Egypt, 1974-86," Cairo Demographic Centre, *Working Paper* 4 (1987), p. 59.
17. *Arab News*, 23 February 1987; *al-Khaleej*, 10 November 1989.
18. WB, *World Tables, 1989-90 Edition*, Baltimore and London: Johns Hopkins University Press, 1990, pp. 226-27, 334-35, 346-47, 546-47, 582-83.

6

The Decline of the Arab Economic Boycott

THE DEVELOPMENT OF THE BOYCOTT

The use of an economic boycott as a weapon by the Arab states against the Yishuv (the pre-state Jewish commvnity in Palestine) preceded the actual military conflict that broke out between them in 1948. The Alexandria Protocol of 1944, which led to the foundation of the Arab League a year later (its signatories being Egypt, Jordan, Syria, Lebanon, Saudi Arabia, Iraq and Yemen, as well as Palestinian representatives), defined one of the goals of the new body as obstructing Jewish economic development in Palestine throvgh the boycott of "Zionist produce." Two years later, in 1946, the League implemented this goal by adopting Resolution 16, which stated that "products of Palestinian Jews are to be considered undesirable in Arab countries. They should be prohibited and refused as long as their production in Palestine might lead to the realization of Zionist political aims."[1] To ensure that Resolution 16 would be effectively applied, the League established a Central Boycott Office which began operating almost immediately from Cairo. The resolution and the executive bodies created in 1946 to implement it provided the basis for the economic warfare the Arab states were to conduct against Israel for decades thereafter.

Apart from the trade carried on between Jews and Arabs within the Palestinian economy itself, the extent of the boycott could only have been very limited. Where the Jewish sector alone was concerned, only ca. 4 percent of total imports came from neighboring Arab markets while only ca. 1 percent of total exports

103

went there. Overall trade ties of the Palestinian economy (Arab and Jewish sectors and direct transactions of the Mandatory government) with the other Middle East economies (including Turkey and Iran) amounted to ca. 20 percent of its total imports and ca. 12 percent of its total exports during 1936–39.[2]

With the Arab political and military failure to prevent the creation of the Jewish state in the late 1940s, Arab opposition to Israel focused on intensified economic warfare. The flow of oil from the Iraq Petroleum Company (IPC) oil fields in Iraq to the refineries in Haifa (owned then by an Anglo-French company) was cut off in 1948 by order of the Iraqi government, with the 1,100-km. pipeline from Kirkuk to Haifa remaining in disuse ever since. Egypt contributed to the economic campaign in the early 1950s by closing the Suez Canal to Israeli merchant vessels and foreign ships carrying cargo bound for Israel, as well as by mounting a blockade in the Gulf of 'Aqaba against merchant ships sailing to Eilat. Syria and Jordan formally rejected cooperation with Israel to exploit the Jordan River waters by means of the Johnston Plan, and although Jordan in fact took steps to implement the plan, Syria, with the backing of the Arab League, initiated a "Jordan sources diversion project" (of the Baniyas and Hasbani Rivers) — an act that led to a serious heightening of tension in Israel's relations with Syria and subsequently in its relations with other Arab states.

Meanwhile, the trade boycott intensified during the early 1950s when it was extended to "third parties," that is, it changed from a bilateral embargo (Israel and the Arab states) to an embargo that functioned in three spheres. The first was an overt and declared embargo (in theory, at least) of any company or individual maintaining economic relations with Israel in commerce, services and the inflow of capital. The second sphere was the economic penalization of individuals and firms that supported Israel politically or acted to foster its economic development. The third sphere was avoiding commercial contracts with Jews or with companies managed by Jewish directors. A different division, into categories of sanctions, consisted of a primary boycott between the conflicting states (the Arab states and Israel) directly; a secondary boycott against any third party maintaining direct economic ties with the banned party (Israel); a tertiary boycott against any third party supporting and assisting the banned party; and a quaternary boycott against any third party with a common religio-national background with the banned party.[3]

The Arab proponents of economic warfare set great store by the embargo during the 1950s. Butros-Ghali, in an article published in 1954, wrote that Arab leaders hoped that the economic boycott would cause the "economic collapse" of the State of Israel, thereby proving that Israel was incapable of surviving economically in a world (i.e., the Arab states) that was hostile to it.[4] Arab League spokesmen justified the widening of the circle of third parties under boycott with the argument that inasmuch as economic health was an important element of national strength, including military power, whoever maintained economic relations with Israel was reinforcing the country militarily and deserved sanctions.[5] Similarly, sanctions were imposed against Jews on the basis of the rationale, articulated succinctly by King Faysal, ruler of Saudi Arabia, that "unfortunately, Jews support Israel, and we regard those who provide aid to our enemies as our own enemies."[6]

These attitudes were crystallized in Resolution 849 of the Arab League Council of December 1954, whose principal points were:

(1) Nationals of member states of the Arab League are prohibited from conducting any kind of transaction, directly or indirectly, with an individual or organization located in Israel or connected with Israel by nationality or acting on behalf of or for Israel, wherever its residence or business premises may be.

(2) The import of Israeli goods by member states of the League is forbidden. This prohibition includes goods produced outside Israel but which contain components or parts of Israeli manufacture or manufactured by Israelis wherever they may be.

(3) Foreign companies having offices, branches or agencies in Israel are included in the prohibition against contracts of any kind with Israel (clause 1 above).

(4) All goods bound for Israel or for individuals and companies mentioned in one of the preceding clauses are considered Israeli goods. As such, dealing in these goods or permitting their transit through Arab territories is prohibited.[7]

In order to implement these decisions, the Boycott Office, which was transferred from Cairo to Damascus in 1949, set about compiling blacklists of industrial enterprises, banks, insurance companies, shipping firms, airlines, film actors and so forth, with whom economic and other links were forbidden. Offices were set up in all League member states, along with a network of boycott bureaus throughout Europe, North America, Latin America, Africa and the Far East, to prepare the lists and enforce the ban. Over the years, the list of "third-party" companies grew longer, from a few hundred in the 1950s to thousands by the late 1970s. A considerable proportion of these parties were American companies and individual American nationals. In 1976 there were 1,500 individual American nationals alone who were listed.[8]

Many companies were effectively banned by all or most of the League members. While statistical information is unavailable, the application of the boycott was undoubtedly widespread in the Arab countries from the 1950s to the late 1970s, especially in Egypt under Nasser, Syria and Iraq under the Ba'th regimes and to a large extent even previously, Libya under Qadhdhafi, and Saudi Arabia under Faysal (1964–75). Only a small number of Arab states did not display particular enthusiasm for the boycott, especially Tunisia and Morocco. For the most part, application was discreet, as the Boycott Office quickly learned that undue exposure jeopardized the effectiveness of the ban. The issue was generally unpopular in the West, and several cases that were brought to the attention of the public by the Israeli government, Jewish organizations or the press in the United States and elsewhere evoked protest.

Examples involving well-known firms illustrate the workings of the boycott. In 1957 Air France was placed on the blacklist because of a charter arrangement with Israel's national airline, El Al, involving several aircraft. That same year the French automobile company Renault was threatened with sanctions in Arab countries if it carried out its intention to construct an assembly plant in Israel. The American fleet added the "Haifa clause" to contracts it signed with oil-supply tankers during 1957–60, which allowed the fleet authorities to cancel contracts with tankers that were prohibited by the Arab Boycott Office from docking at Arab harbors because they had previously called at the port of Haifa. The British insurance firm Norwich Union was placed under threat of boycott in 1961 because its director, Lord Mancroft, was a Jew who did not conceal his sympathy for Israel. Lord Mancroft resigned. In 1965 a three-month ban was imposed on the British conglomerate Imperial Chemical Industries (ICI) and its 77 subsidiaries because they marketed products in Israel. The following year Coca-Cola was blacklisted because the company had yielded to Jewish and other pressure to license the opening of a soft-drink plant in Israel. Another multinational that joined the blacklist in 1966 was Ford when it announced a plan to set up an assembly plant in Israel. Radio Corporation of America

(RCA) was put on the list too. Other prominent multinational companies that were added to the list during the 1960s were Sony of Japan and British Leyland. The a priori submission of the large Japanese automobile firms to the boycott conditions up until the 1980s was evident, with Subaru the only such company to ignore the boycott and market in Israel (becoming a favorite of Israeli car purchasers).[9]

Two particularly successful periods in the history of the embargo were the peak years of messianic Nasserism (1957–66), and the period between the first and second oil crises of the 1970s (1973–79), when the rise in importance of Middle Eastern oil in the world economy undoubtedly contributed to the effectiveness of the boycott.

The Boycott Office followed these procedures: (1) lobbying and pressuring companies to prevent them from forming economic ties with Israel before such ties were actually made (typical of contacts with Japanese companies); (2) threatening to blacklist companies that had decided to establish ties with Israel but had not yet implemented their plans (the policy adopted in respect of many Western companies); (3) blacklisting companies but not actually enforcing the boycott, while exerting heavy pressure on the companies to halt their trade with Israel; and (4) applying the boycott in practice, with an assurance that it would be lifted the moment direct or indirect ties with Israel were severed. As oil income rose, the Arab oil states expanded acquisitions of goods and services from foreign firms considerably, thereby heightening the effectiveness of the boycott threat.

It was precisely the relative success of the Boycott Office that eventually motivated American companies to take stronger measures to oppose it.[10] These were adopted by Congress and the Ford Administration in Washington during 1975–77 following approaches by the Israeli government, which in 1976 established a Finance Ministry unit to counter economic warfare, although the most persuasive factor was Jewish and general public opinion in the United States which focused on the threat to American values posed by the Arab Boycott Office. In 1975 the US Secretary of Commerce announced that American firms were prohibited from discriminating in commercial contracts on the basis of "race, color, religion, sex or national origin," and ordered all companies to report instances where they had come under economic boycott pressure and what their response to such pressure had been.[11] In 1976, Congress passed the Tax Reform Act, and, even more

THE MIDDLE EAST OIL DECADE AND BEYOND

significantly, added amendments to the Export Administration Act in 1977 (PL 95-52), which made compliance by a company or an individual to the application of an economic boycott illegal and empowered the courts to impose heavy penalties for infringing this law.[12]

This series of measures seriously impeded Boycott Office operations in the United States, with the number of American companies that succumbed to pressures and threats by the office falling markedly, although compliance did not disappear.[13] No other country took steps as far-reaching or effective, although political leaders in Canada, France and Holland condemned the boycott publicly.[14] While these condemnations had only little practical results, they reflected the displeasure of a substantial segment of the public in these democratic societies at measures taken by foreigners to influence their own economic activity.

THE DECLINE OF THE SECONDARY BOYCOTT

In the event, despite limited international counteraction, the effectiveness of the boycott gradually declined from the start of the 1980s onward for a variety of reasons:

(1) With the reduction of Arab oil power, the Boycott Office lost leverage in the industrialized countries. Neither the enticements nor the risks were as great as they had been in the 1970s, and companies in Japan or in Europe were no longer as responsive to the demands of the boycott apparatus.

(2) Concomitantly, the Israeli market was growing, its public having acquired the consumption patterns of an affluent society by the 1980s. The loss of this market was less acceptable to foreign companies, including multinationals, than previously.

(3) Egypt, which had led the Arab states in the struggle against Israel during the 1950s and 1960s, withdrew from the conflict. The peace agreement also terminated Egypt's role in the economic boycott. Significantly, Coca-Cola, the symbol of the effectiveness of the ban, resumed the marketing of its products in Egypt vigorously. Once breached, the boycott was difficult to maintain, particularly in the Maghreb, where countries that had previously been lax in applying the boycott rules regarding third parties were even less inclined to apply the blacklists drawn up in the 1980s.

(4) The strengthening of ties between several of the Arab states

and the United States and other Western countries at the end of the 1970s and during the 1980s further impeded the effectiveness of the boycott. Inasmuch as the boycott was considered an inappropriate obstacle by the Western economies, once the Western and Arab economic and political frameworks began to converge, the boycott was increasingly difficult to implement both domestically and abroad.

(5) The atmosphere throughout the world during the *glasnost* years and the great thaw between the world blocs was less tolerant of the insular patterns of relations that were characteristic of the Cold War era. Like other barriers, the boycott became largely anachronistic in a global political and economic system striving to tear down walls and breach divisive boundaries.

(6) The growing worldwide tendency toward subcontracting in the manufacturing process during the 1980s, obstructed the application of the boycott. With the production of a single item likely to involve dozens of subcontractors on two or three continents, and the label "Made in" relating only to the final stage of the production process, the Boycott Office and the Arab governments discovered that it was virtually impossible to identify goods with Israeli components. Even when such components were detected, the consumers, namely Arab governments, were not willing to forgo acquiring them when there were no suitable or acceptable alternatives, for example in the area of US-manufactured arms.[15]

(7) The amount of goods and services imported by Israel in the 1980s consistently grew, as did the number of foreign companies trading with Israel, causing an unwieldy expansion of the blacklists. The Boycott Office was therefore obliged to become increasingly selective in its decisions, and this involved great difficulties.

(8) The developments outlined above took place during a period — the 1980s — when resources available to the Boycott Office in Damascus and the coordinating bureaus abroad were dwindling.[16] Recessions in the Persian Gulf oil states — the chief contributors to the Arab League treasury; the drain on finances owing to assistance granted to Iraq in its war with Iran; and the absence of Egypt's participation in the League during most of the decade resulted in a period of hardship for the Arab League and its institutions, including the Boycott Office. Moreover, the ever-decreasing sums allocated by the League Council to the Boycott Office seemed to reflect a reduction in the status of the

office and in the importance attached to its work during the decade.

(9) There was a change in the Arab view of economic warfare during the late 1980s, questioning the purpose and wisdom of the very existence of the boycott. If the point of the boycott had originally been to cause the economic collapse of Israel, by the 1980s the growing discrepancy between the goal and the practical results of the boycott could not be ignored. Varying estimates exist as to the cost the boycott exacted from the Israeli economy, but even the most partisan supporters of economic warfare against Israel were forced to admit that at its most successful the boycott came nowhere near realizing its goal of bringing about the economic collapse of Israel.

Questions arose in the 1980s not only regarding the purpose of the boycott, but regarding the wisdom of the use of this weapon as well, in view of indications that the boycott had actually acted as a spur to the development of the Israeli economy. Just as the ongoing military threat and the uncertain supply of foreign arms promoted the development of Israel's military and air industries, so economic warfare ultimately contributed to the development of a range of Israeli civilian industries serving as a protective barrier against imports. For example, the fact that foreign soft drink manufacturers (Coca-Cola, Schweppes and others) had not marketed their products in Israel for about twenty years made it possible for local companies to become established (Tempo, Tavori, Assis, etc.). While this view of the effects or consequences of the boycott has not yet been comprehensively researched, it is noteworthy that such evaluations of the boycott and its results were prevalent as far back as the late 1960s,[17] and it is reasonable to assume that they affected official positions in the Arab countries. Equally relevant, calculations of the economic harm caused by the boycott to Israel show limited damage. According to one calculation, the cost to the Israeli economy resulting from the restricted range of imports amounted to an average of $44 million annually between 1951 and 1980.[18] In drawing up a balance sheet of the costs of the economic warfare campaign, the price of the boycott to the Arab League and its member states must be subtracted from the cost to the Israeli economy. While there are no available figures for the operating costs of the boycott apparatus or the losses to the Arab states as a result of lack of commercial activity by boycotted foreign companies, clearly the balance of and the benefits of the costs of the Israel–Arab economic war was not favorable to the proponents of this weapon.

By the 1980s, the Boycott Office had lost much of its thrust. Staff members of the office themselves admitted that the effectiveness of the operation had declined and that boycott barriers were ruptured in numerous areas.[19] It became increasingly clear that foreign firms that had feared retaliatory measures by the Boycott Office in the past now ignored it, while Arab governments, excluding Egypt, tended to be less cooperative and to bypass decisions made by the office if the boycott of a foreign company might hinder development projects or other transactions deemed vital. Evidence of the breakdown of the effectiveness of the boycott was obvious at the busy container terminals at Israeli ports. A long list of firms that had previously forfeited the Israeli market, especially Japanese firms, began to export to Israel in the 1980s. Some did so directly, while others adopted methods developed in the 1950s and 1960s of exporting through subsidiaries or straw companies. The resultant availability of a wide range of imported goods in Israel became immediately obvious.[20]

Nevertheless, the Boycott Office continued operating, its network of offices and bureaus in the Arab states and throughout the world still functioned in the early 1990s. The blacklists were followed up and updated.[21] But matters no longer proceeded as in the 1960s and 1970s. The prevalent feeling both in Israel and in Arab League circles was that this means, which had been intended to drastically reduce, if not entirely prevent, economic ties between Israel and third parties, had become ineffective. The unit in the Israeli Finance Ministry to counter economic warfare was reduced in size. Reports in the early 1990s from Israeli businessmen presented a similar picture. The boycott existed, but its actual effect regarding ties with third parties had shrunk.

The continued existence of the Boycott Office presumably might have been justified if the ban on direct links between Israel and the Arab states themselves had remained in force. But matters turned out otherwise. From the 1970s onward, the Boycott Office became aware that in this area too cracks had appeared in the wall which were steadily widening.

THE DECLINE OF THE PRIMARY BOYCOTT

The first significant crack in the wall of the Arab boycott erected to prevent Israeli-produced goods from entering Arab economies followed the Israeli occupation of the West Bank in the 1967 war. In a matter of months after the war had ended, the occupied territories began to serve as a channel for the export of Israeli produce to Arab states east of the Jordan River. At first the exported goods consisted entirely of agricultural produce, but soon industrial goods were exported as well. The Jordanian authorities in charge of commerce and the Boycott Office in Amman became aware of this development, and by the end of the 1960s certification was required from chambers of commerce in the West Bank towns and the Gaza Strip that the origin of every item destined for Jordan and further east was Palestinian Arab. However, Israeli businessmen, both Jews and Arabs, found ways of circumventing this requirement, while officials in the West Bank chambers of commerce did not always implement the inspections rigidly.

Another route for the export of Israeli goods to Arab economies, principally to Lebanon and Syria, opened up in 1975 when direct connections with the residents of southern Lebanon were initiated. Again, agricultural produce constituted the initial exports, to be followed by processed foodstuffs, household items and eventually a wide range of Israeli manufactured goods.

A further development occurred toward the end of the 1970s when the Arab oil states and adjoining countries such as Jordan experienced a peak in consumer consumption as a result of the steep rise in income from oil exports, while at the same time Israeli exporters, having lost the Iranian market after the collapse of the Pahlavi regime, were searching for alternative outlets. The logical solution for the Israeli exporters was the neighboring Arab countries. Existing channels expanded and new ones developed, especially in export arrangements by means of a third party — straw companies in Cyprus, Greece, Spain and elsewhere. Israeli companies took precautions to conceal the origin of the goods they exported, while some firms went a step further by packaging their products to suit the taste of Arab consumers.

The first published estimates on the scope of Israeli-Arab commerce (excluding Israeli exports to the West Bank and the Gaza Strip) appeared in the early 1980s, indicating about $500 million in 1980 prices.[22] This figure is most probably an over-estimation. In fact, the various estimates were not based on official figures, as the Israeli Central Bureau of Statistics (CBS) did not publish data on the extent of Israeli-Arab trade or on any other aspect of economic relations between Israel and its

Arab neighbors. The policy of the CBS was apparently motivated by two factors. First, economic ties between Israel and the Arab countries (apart from relations with Egypt from 1979 onward) did not formally exist, and publication of data by the CBS would imply otherwise. Secondly, a large proportion of Israeli goods reached Arab countries via a transit destination, so that gathering data was bound to be a complex and inexact procedure, given that cooperation on the part of the Israeli producer-exporter would probably not be obtainable. This problem was ongoing so long as trade had to be conducted under the shadow of the Boycott Office and other hindrances arising from political and ideological considerations.

The overall value of Israeli exports to Arab countries therefore has to be assessed on the basis of estimated data on type of goods exported, quantity and market prices. Since data for quantity are based entirely on estimates, figures should be regarded only as approximations.

The next stage in the development of trade ties resulted from the establishment of formal peace relations between Israel and Egypt in 1979. However, while formal commercial relations were initiated between the two states, the volume of trade, apart from the export of oil from Egypt to Israel, was limited. In 1988 and 1989 total Israeli exports to Egypt amounted to an average of only about $31 million, mainly comprising refined oil products. If indirect exports of refined products are included in the total commercial export to Egypt, then the figure was about $55 million in those years.[23]

Paradoxically, the volume of exports to other Arab economies, especially those east of the Jordan River, underwent incomparably more impressive growth during the 1980s. Goods exported were highly varied and included fresh and frozen fruits and vegetables, processed foods, textiles, office equipment, furniture, cosmetics and pharmaceutical goods, agricultural equipment (especially drip irrigation systems, seeds, pesticides and fertilizers), electrical appliances (especially communications equipment and air-conditioners), vehicle parts and tires.[24] The total value of exports to all the Arab states (including Egypt and the North African countries) probably amounted to $200–300 million in the late 1980.[25]

If, however, Israeli exports to Arab countries grew, the import of products from Arab countries to Israel, excluding crude oil from Egypt, remained minimal. From 1979, when the oil trade between

113

Egypt and Israel began, to the end of 1989, Israel purchased crude oil from Egypt worth about $3.9 billion overall (current prices), or about $350 million annually, constituting roughly 25 percent of Israel's total expenditure for crude oil purchases in that period.[26]

The composition of the basket of products that the Arab states (together) imported from Israeli producers is a good indicator of the forces that propelled this trade from the start. In this context the basket may be divided into two main groups: agricultural, electronics and communications equipment; and foodstuffs and consumer goods. The first group was characterized by qualitative advantages in the Arab markets, namely superiority to alternative products made elsewhere in terms of suitability to environmental conditions (climate, water), fulfilling specific needs or satisfying customers' tastes. In some categories, the advantages of Israeli products were so obvious that they faced no real competition, for example, in the area of sophisticated agricultural equipment. By 1990 the acquisition of Israeli-made goods of this kind by buyers in Arab countries was no longer a secret. The Israeli Agritech exhibitions held in Tel Aviv in the late 1980s attracted businessmen representing Saudi Arabia, Iraq, Syria, Lebanon, Jordan and the Maghreb states. These buyers came to the exhibition at the invitation of local Israeli manufacturers who had maintained ongoing trade ties with them for years.[27]

Commerce in the second group of goods — foodstuffs and consumer products — developed as a result of the advantages of border trade, or trade between neighbors, namely, the relatively low costs of packaging, shipping and insurance. These advantages were particularly attractive in the final costing of bulky goods such as fresh food, or furniture. Moreover, certain goods in this category — clothing, furniture and household utensils — which were marketed to a wide range of populations, could be easily adapted to varying requirements during the production process.

The common denominator that promoted trade in both groups of commodities was the regional element, namely, the advantages resulting from the producer and the consumer belonging to the same geo-economic area. This was self-evident in terms of border trade but was no less valuable in relation to specialized trade as well, where similar regional conditions converted the manufacturer, the product and the consumer into a cohesive economic-commercial complex. That the regional common denominator was a compelling force was attested by the fact that a variety of commercial ties were developed despite almost total economic and political separation.

It is reasonable to assume that the removal of these barriers and the opening up of boundaries will result in an expansion of both border trade and specialized trade.

Available information indicates that both sides profited from the existing trade, both in the macro-economic and macro-social respect. Since trade was conducted in spheres where the importing state had no production capability of its own (for the Arab states, the specialized items; for Israel, crude oil), or where domestic demand created a market for import (accounting for the border trade, such as foodstuffs), it did not force local producers out of the market. Partial evidence supporting this conclusion may be found in the fact that despite the growth in imports of Israeli-produced goods, there were no complaints from either Arab farmers or Arab domestic manufacturers. Moreover, the development of this trade was not associated with any social cost. Quite the contrary, it may be reasonably expected that some of this commerce produced social benefits in that agricultural equipment aimed at expanding cultivated areas and working existing areas more efficiently ultimately helped slow down rural–urban migration or reduce open and hidden unemployment in the villages themselves.

The movement of goods between Israel and the Arab states was, in fact, a clear example of F.A. Hayek's definition of a "spontaneous [economic] order" which is a function of "human activity, and not of any human design."[28] The phenomenon stemmed solely from the motivation of interested parties on both sides of the political border seeking higher incomes and profits. Significantly, not only did this "spontaneous order" not conflict with the general economic interest, it permitted the population, or a part of it, to raise productivity (in agriculture, for example) and provided a choice of cheaper or more varied products, similar or identical in quality, at no social cost. Hence, this trade made a positive contribution to the public in general, above and beyond the profits it provided for the entrepreneurs, manufacturers and merchants engaged in it.

Two aspects of this situation deserve special notice. First, advantages existed in the fact that the beginnings of inter-state Israeli-Arab trade were taking place in conditions of closed borders and the absence of normal political relations, as trade proceeded without political interference. The low visibility of these ties freed them from obstruction on ideological or political grounds. This "hidden" advantage, however, was far outweighed by the advantages of open and overt commerce. Second, there are grounds for arguing that the boycott contributed to the development of the Israeli economy along lines that eventually made it complementary to rather than competitive with the Arab economies, especially in terms of industrial manufacture. Denied the possibility of exporting to neighboring states, Israeli industrialists had to compete in Western markets. Israeli industry developed accordingly, and the long years when the movement of Israeli goods eastward was blocked were years when the foundations were laid in Israel for sophisticated and specialized industries. By the time the trade encounter between the Arab and Israeli economies occurred in the 1970s and 1980s, Israel's industry had a range of goods to offer that not only were not produced in the Arab states but were competitive in any market. Hence, the basis for developed and diversified trade relations between Israel and the Arab economies was created.

NOTES

1. B.Y. Boutros-Ghali, "The Arab League: Ten Years of Struggle," *International Conciliation*, May 1954: 408 (hereafter: Boutros-Ghali).
2. Government of Palestine, Departments of Statistics, *Statistics of Foreign Trade 1944 & 1945*, p. 00.
3. For a somewhat different categorization see Henry J. Steiner, "International Boycotts and Domestic Order: American Involvement in the Arab Israeli Conflict," *Texas Law Review* 54/7 (1976): 1367-70; Howard Stanislawki, "The Impact of the Arab Boycott of Israel on the United States and Canada" in David Leyton-Brown (ed.), *The Utility of International Economic Sanctions*, London and Sydney: Croom Helm, 1987, pp. 224-25 (hereafter: Stanislawski).
4. Boutros-Ghali, p. 421.
5. Robert W. MacDonald, *The League of Arab States: A Study of the Dynamics of Regional Organization*, Princeton: Princeton University Press, 1965, pp. 122-23 (hereafter: MacDonald).
6. Donald L. Losman, *International Economic Sanctions: The Cases of Cuba, Israel and Rhodesia*, Albuquerque: University of New Mexico Press, 1979, p. 60 (hereafter: Losman).
7. Andreas F. Lowenfeld, "...'Sauce for the Gander': The Arab Boycott and United States Political Trade Controls," *Texas International Law Journal* 12 (1977): 26-27 (hereafter: Lowenfeld).
8. Losman, ibid.; cf. Dan S. Chill, *The Arab Boycott of Israel: Economic Aggression and World Reaction*, New York: Praeger, 1976, p. 53.
9. MacDonald, p. 120; Losman, pp. 58-62; W.H. Nelson and T. Prittle, *The Economic War against the Jews*, New York: Random House, 1977, pp. 50-57; Margaret P. Doxey, *Economic Santions and International Enforcement*, 2nd ed., London: Macmillan, 1980, pp. 21-22.
10. *New York Times*, 17 January 1976.
11. US Department of Commerce, *Export Administration Report*, 116th Repprt on US Export Controls to the President and the Congress, April-September 1977.

12. Lowenfeld, pp. 36-37; Stanislawski, pp. 229-35.
13. Stanislawski, pp. 235-38; *Ma'ariv* ('Asaqim), 28 November 1989.
14. Namey Turck, "A Comparative Study of Non-United States Responses to the Arab Boycott," *Georgia Journal of International and Comparative Law* 8 (1978): 714-15, 726; Stanislawski, pp. 238-49.
15. *Ma'ariv*, 26 February 1990.
16. *al-Majalla al-Iqtisadiyya* (London), 22 November 1988.
17. Frank Gervasi, *The Case for Israel*, New York: Viking Press, 1967, p. 134.
18. Gary Clyde Hufbauer and Jeffrey J. Schott, *Economic Sanctions Reconsidered: History and Current Policy*, Washington DC: Institute for International Economics, 1985, pp. 183-84. See also Gardner Patterson, "Israel's Economic Problems," *Foreign Affairs* 32 (January 1954): 321; Harry Ellis, *Israel and the Middle East*, New York: Ronald Press, 1957, p. 162.
19. *Arab News*, 28 January 1983; *Khaleej Times*, 25 February 1983; *al-Majalla al-Iqtisadiyya* (London), 22 November 1988.
20. In the 1980s several major Japanese cars and electronic corporations sold their products in Israel.
21. *Emirates News*, 21 November 1988; *al-Qabas*, 13 January 1989; *Khaleej Times*, 6 March 1989.
22. Hesh Kestin, "Israel's best-kept secret," *Forbes*, 22 October 1984.
23. Government of Israel, Central Bureau of Statistics.
24. *al-Ittihad* (Abu Dhabi), 14 May 1984, 17 November 1988; *al-Safir*, 2 October 1986; *al-Majalla al-Iqtisadiyya* (London), 22 November 1988; *Arab Times*, 2 April 1989.
25. Cf. *Financial Times*, 6 July 1989.
26. Government of Israel, Bank of Israel.
27. *Ma'ariv*, 3 January 1990.
28. See F.A. Hayek, *Studies in Philosophy, Politics and Economics*, London: Routledge and Kegan Paul, 1967, pp. 162-63 ff.

Index